Table of Contents

ENVIRONMENTAL ISSUES

All living things need an environment in which to live. Their survival and development depends on the living and non-living factors in their surroundings. Over the last few decades, it has become increasingly evident that human activities are having harmful effects on our natural environment. Scientific understanding of the Earth and its ecosystems has increased significantly in recent years. Environmental science is now a major interdisciplinary academic study attempting to assess risks and solutions. Individuals, businesses, governments and multinational organizations increasingly recognize that actions must be taken to protect the environment, both for its own sake and for the benefit of humans inhabiting that environment. There are a large number of **environmental issues**.

Environmental problems are often ethical problems. Some people believe that environmental issues matter only when they are harmful to humans. For example, pollution only becomes an ethical issue when it is harmful to human health. But, even this human-centred view raises many ethical questions.

Is it morally wrong to burn fossil fuels knowing that it causes harmful pollution and climate change?

How do we share out the costs and benefits of protecting the environment?

Do we have a moral duty to conserve resources for future generations?

How do we balance what people want in developed countries against what people need in developing countries?

5

However, many people think that other species and the rest of the natural world matter for their own sakes regardless of their usefulness to humans. There is widespread disagreement about what is morally right or wrong with regard to the environment. Reasonable people who would probably regard themselves as ethical can come to quite different conclusions with respect to environmental issues. So, it is not enough to claim that something is right or wrong. We also have to explain why we think so.

Ethics is the study of the concepts involved in deciding what we should do, or what sort of person we should be. Ethics includes the attempt to devise standards and principles to guide our behaviour. What is the right, or wrong, way to behave? How should we think about the consequences of our actions? What duties or obligations should we accept? What characteristic behaviours should we cultivate in ourselves?

Environmental ethics is concerned with ethical questions specifically in relationship to the environment. How should we behave with respect to the natural world, its resources, and non-human inhabitants? Do the consequences of our actions on the environment or other species matter? Do we have any duties or obligations towards the environment or other species? Should we cultivate environmentally friendly behaviours in ourselves?

Ethical questions are unavoidable. Some might argue that environmental issues are not ethical issues. They are merely problems to be solved by economics, or science and technology. But that itself would be an ethical decision. It assumes that the value of non-human entities can be expressed in terms of their usefulness to humans, and that is an ethical viewpoint that not everyone accepts. So, it has to be justified. Whatever our attitudes to the environment may be, we cannot avoid facing ethical questions concerning the natural world and its non-human inhabitants.

There is not yet a unified theory of ethics, however. There are various conflicting theories that can give conflicting answers to environmental questions. This is a particular problem for theories in the western philosophical tradition that began in ancient Greece. Western ethical theories have been concerned only with human relations and have tended to neglect our relations with the environment and its non-human inhabitants.

Ethical theories have been described as *'research programmes'*. Each programme can provide a useful approach to thinking about ethical problems, but no one theory yet has all the answers. This book will describe some ethical approaches, their achievements so far in investigating environmental problems, and the questions that each still has to answer.

MORAL STATUS

One question that all theories have to answer is, **what has moral status**? If it matters how something is treated, we say that it has moral status. (This might be expressed in various equivalent ways: it has moral standing, moral considerability, it deserves moral consideration and so on). If something has moral status then we have a moral obligation to consider the effects of our decisions on it, for its own sake, regardless of any benefits to ourselves. Our answers to environmental questions therefore depend on what we think has moral status. What is the scope of moral status? Where do we draw the line between what has and what does not have moral status?

If only humans have moral status then whether actions that affect the environment are morally right or wrong depends only on their effect on humans

But, if non-human species and the rest of nature have moral status then we have to take into account effects on them as well

MORAL STATUS

The Last Man Argument

The last man argument provides a way to think about what has moral status. Richard Routley proposed a thought experiment where we imagine that there is only one man left alive on the planet. This last man on earth has the technology to destroy all other living things after he has died. He can even ensure that the entire planet will be destroyed after he has gone.

If the last man destroys the planet, has he done anything wrong?

Instrumental versus Intrinsic Value

If we think in terms of traditional ethical theories it would be difficult to say that the last man has done anything wrong. Traditional theories assume that only humans have value. That is, only humans need to be taken into consideration when making decisions. The last man has not harmed any other humans. So, he has done nothing wrong.

But, many people feel that needlessly destroying the planet and all other living things would be wrong. So, is it correct to assume that only humans have value? Early debates in environmental ethics were often about whether other species and the rest of the natural world have value, and if so what kind of value. Do they have *instrumental* or *intrinsic* value?

The natural world had only *instrumental value*. It could be used as an 'instrument' to achieve something else. If there are no humans left to make use of nature then it no longer has any value. So, the last man did nothing wrong

But many people think that the world has **intrinsic value**. Living things and the environment are valuable for their own sakes, regardless of their usefulness to others. So, the last man did do something wrong

Subjective Intrinsic Value

Instrumental versus intrinsic value is now seen as a ***false choice***. They are not the only possibilities. It was thought that intrinsic value is ***objective***. An inherent property of a thing, not dependent on our subjective feelings. However, it has proven difficult to identify an uncontroversial inherent property that justifies moral status, or even to prove that such a thing exists. It is now widely accepted that some things can have ***subjective intrinsic value***. We can value some things simply for their own sakes, regardless of their usefulness, or any intrinsic property we believe they may have. For example, we might value a beautiful sunset. It is not obviously useful, nor does it have any obvious inherently valuable property. So, we value a sunset for its own sake. But that value is also subjective. It arises from within ourselves.

Interests

Alternatively, some have argued that *interests* might provide objective intrinsic value. We have an interest in something if that something can make our lives go better or worse. Some interests are *instrumental*, we need them to achieve our goals. But some interests are *essential*. For example, food and water are essential to our physical survival.

Some argue that possession of essential interests justifies moral status. Certain essential interests may be considered to matter morally. Harming those interests would be morally wrong. So, entities that possess those interests have moral status. The traditional view was that only human interests matter. But, many entities possess essential interests. Many environmental philosophers argue that these non-human essential interests matter as well. The scope of moral status thus depends on which interests we think should be taken into account. For example, if we believe that an interest in survival is morally significant then perhaps all living things should have moral status.

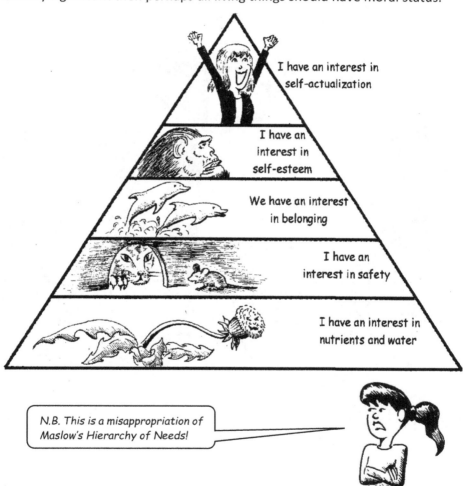

Extending the Scope of Moral Status

Some environmental philosophers argue that the last man argument shows that we need a radical new ethical theory. But, others argue that traditional theories can be extended to include non-human entities. The problem is that traditional theories have assumed that only humans have moral status. But, if we extend the scope of moral status to include non-human entities, then traditional theories will be able to tell us what to do. However, there is disagreement over how far we can or should extend the scope of moral status. Our choice of what to include within the scope of moral status will influence the type of ethical approach that we adopt.

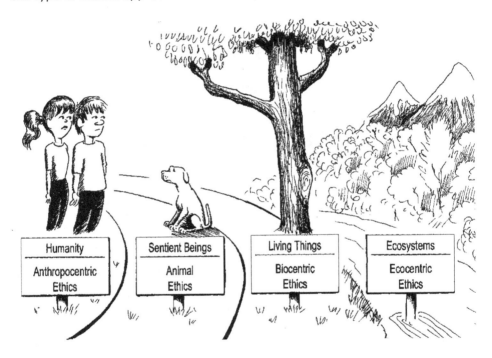

ANTHROPOCENTRIC ETHICS

Anthropocentrism views humans as the only entities that have moral status. Only humans have intrinsic value. Human interests are the only interests that matter. Any interests that non-human entities may possess are not significant. Other living things and the environment may have at most instrumental value.

Anthropocentric ethics is concerned only with human well-being. It is not concerned with effects on non-human living things or the rest of nature, except when those effects may cause indirect harm to other humans. Nevertheless, many environmental issues have harmful effects on humans. So, even anthropocentric ethics justifies some moral concern for the environment.

Anthropocentrism

Anthropocentrism is embedded in traditional western ethics, from ancient Greek philosophers through medieval and into modern philosophy.

> Nature has made all things specifically for the sake of man

Aristotle (384 – 322 BC)

> Non-human animals are intended for man's use... Hence it is not wrong for man to make use of them, either by killing or using them in any other way whatsoever

Thomas Aquinas (1225 – 1274)

> Animals are machines; speech is the only certain sign of thought; only humans can speak; so, animals are unlikely to have minds. Nature can produce automata and these natural automata are the animals

René Descartes (1596 – 1650)

There were some exceptions ...

Be praised, my Lord, through all Your creatures

Unity of nature means that everything is connected to everything else

St Francis of Assisi (1181/1182 – 1226)

Baruch Spinoza (1632 – 1677)

... and science now recognizes the connections between humans and the rest of nature.

Let it be borne in mind how infinitely complex and close-fitting are the mutual relations of all organic beings to each other and to their physical conditions of life

Charles Darwin

(1809 – 1882)

N.B. "survival of the fittest" was first used by **Herbert Spencer (1820 – 1903)**, now best known for 'social darwinism' which applies the law of survival of the fittest to society.

How often misused words generate misleading thoughts

However, western ethical theories, have traditionally been anthropocentric.

Human Interests

Anthropocentric ethics is concerned only with **human interests**, things that are important to human flourishing and success. However, many environmental problems do cause significant harms to humans and their interests.

7 million premature deaths annually are linked to air pollution

World Health Organization

Climate change has led to changes in climate extremes such as heat waves, record high temperatures and ... heavy precipitation in the past half century

Intergovernmental Panel on Climate Change

A changing climate will have real impacts on our military and the way it executes its missions

The United States Department of Defence

Identifying and quantifying planetary boundaries that must not be transgressed could help prevent human activities from causing unacceptable environmental change

Stockholm Resilience Centre

Anthropocentric ethics therefore, can justify strict environmental policies. It is morally wrong to cause harm to human interests. Many environmental problems cause harm to human interests. So, causing environmental problems harmful to humans is morally wrong. Avoiding harm to human interests requires sustaining a healthy environment. So, anthropocentric ethics could demand significant improvements to our current treatment of the environment. Decisions that may affect the environment must balance any harmful effects on humans against any expected benefits. This could justify much stricter environmental policies than those we currently see in practice.

21

The natural world has instrumental value because it provides us with medicines, food, raw materials, and perhaps other resources yet to be discovered. Moreover, it is impossible to predict which organisms may be necessary to support the ecosystems that sustain human life. But, something with only instrumental value can be replaced. So, it might be argued that technology could replace the natural world with an artificial environment that would provide all of our material needs.

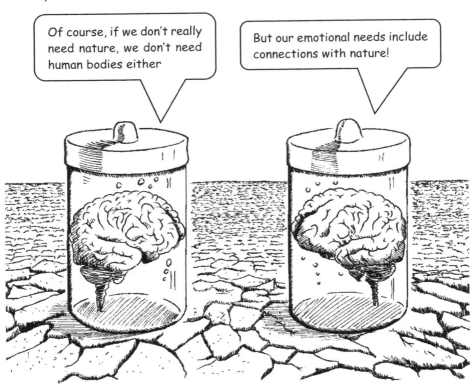

E. O. Wilson argues that nature is important not only for our material needs but also our *emotional needs*. Wilson calls this *biophilia*, the connections that humans subconsciously seek with the rest of life. Humanity is part of nature, one species that evolved among other species. To understand ourselves we need the full biodiversity in which we originated. Moreover, our emotional needs include connections with nature. For example, many people who have the means and the leisure backpack, hunt, fish, go birdwatching or garden.

It might be argued that technology could also replace our emotional needs for connections to nature. For example, if a **virtual reality** machine could provide a convincing illusion of any experience that we could want from nature, then would that provide a satisfactory replacement for the actual natural world?*

Some people might accept being plugged into the machine as an acceptable replacement. But, many people might not. If it is not an acceptable replacement then this seems to suggest that *real* experience of nature, for its own sake, is an important component of well-being for many people.

from an example originally by Robert Nozick

Anthropocentric ethics therefore, can justify concern for nature both for its instrumental value in meeting human material needs, and for its subjective value as an important component of human well-being. As well as appreciating the beauty of nature, many people resent wanton destruction of nature. Many people feel a sense of respect towards cultural artefacts or historical antiquities. Wanton destruction of such valued objects is widely rejected as 'vandalism'. Many people feel a similar sense of respect for nature and would regard the wanton destruction of other species or ecosystems as vandalism. Many people also object to the gratuitous suffering of non-human animals. Although they may believe that non-human animals have less moral value than humans, they may also believe that non-human animals should be treated humanely and that inflicting unnecessary suffering is wrong. Very few would argue that we can do anything we want to non-human animals.

Future generations

Many people also believe that we have obligations to future generations. We should avoid harming the environment because future generations of humans should have the resources they will need for a decent quality of life, and the chance to enjoy nature and see other living things as some of us do today.

Alternatively, some might argue that we have no obligations to future generations because they cannot reciprocate. We can benefit them, but they cannot benefit us in return.

What have future generations ever done for us?

Minister of Old Jokes

But, others might respond that we already respect obligations to people who cannot reciprocate. For example, we respect the wills of dead people.

And finally, I request that my beneficiaries take the same care of the planet that I did

And others respond that although future generations cannot do anything for us, they can do something for their future generations. That is, there is a general form of transgenerational reciprocity where each generation benefits the next generation in return for being benefitted by the previous generation.

The Non-Identity Problem

It might be argued that we do not have obligations to future generations because we do not know who they will be. **Derek Parfit** initially raised this *"non-identity problem"*. Actions taken today will affect who exists in the future. Different policies adopted today may affect who meets whom, and who has children with whom. Different children will be born who will grow up, meet different persons and have different children in turn. After only a few generations entirely different sets of future people will exist. So, one set of environmental policies might lead to one group of future people, while a different set of policies might lead to an entirely different group.

If the identities of future persons depends on our actions today then to whom do we owe moral obligations? Moreover, how could future persons complain about our environmentally destructive policies if they would not have existed without those policies? It might be argued therefore, that disastrous environmental policies do not cause any harm to anyone. Although future persons will lead miserable lives, they would not exist if we did not adopt those policies. So, we have not made them worse off than they would otherwise have been. If this argument is correct then we would have no reason to choose an environmentally friendly policy over a disastrous policy, provided the disastrous effects will not occur for at least a few generations.

Some philosophers accept that the non-identity problem proves that environmentally destructive polices are not morally wrong. But, most continue to feel that it is wrong to pursue policies that will cause future persons to live miserable lives. Unfortunately, it has proven difficult to say exactly why it is wrong. Various possible solutions have been proposed. But, so far, all have met further objections. This debate still continues.

Can acts be wrong even though no future person will be made worse off?

Can acts be wrong without making future persons worse off?

Can acts be wrong if different acts would make future persons better off?

Can acts be wrong if they do not show appropriate moral concern?

Sustainable Development

Another problem is that we do not know what future people might want. Why conserve fuel sources if future people might develop alternative forms of energy generation? Why preserve biodiversity if future people might not be interested in the rest of the natural world?

It may be reasonable to assume that future persons will have similar basic needs, such as food, water and health care. So, we may have moral obligations to leave sufficient resources to meet future basic needs. But, we still do not meet the basic needs of many present day persons. Some critics argue that concern for the needs of future generations compromises our concern to meet the needs of present generations.

The Brundtland Commission, sponsored by the UN, established the concept of *sustainable development*, which is intended to combine environmental protection with economic development and social justice. It acknowledges a moral obligations both to consider the needs of future generations and also to promote present economic development in order to eliminate poverty. It is also a matter of social justice in that it seeks to restrain the rich from their over-consumption of non-renewable resources and to assist the poor in achieving economic development while also protecting the environment. However, how to meet these obligations is still a matter of debate.

Questions for anthropocentric ethics

Are anthropocentric ethics the problem, not the solution?

Lynn White Jr. argued that because we believe that only humans matter, we believe we can dominate, exploit and destroy all other living things. He argues that medieval Judeo-Christian theology was the origin of our belief that the planet is a resource for human consumption. Then the industrial revolution greatly increased our ability to exploit and destroy the environment.

White started a continuing debate about the role of religion in our modern destructive attitudes towards nature. He proposed **St. Francis of Assisi** as a model of respect for nature. We must "rethink and refeel" our attitudes towards nature. We must abandon our superior attitude towards the rest of the world, and follow the example of St Francis in respecting other living things and limiting our rule over the world.

Stewardship

Some critics disagreed with White's analysis of the Bible, and argued that Genesis asserts not dominion but "**stewardship**", which requires that humans are responsible for the world and should take care of it. In 1979, Pope John Paul II declared St. Francis the Patron Saint of Ecology.

We are "not to behave like dissident predators where nature is concerned, but to assume responsibility for it

Questions for Stewardship

Can we assume that we have the right to manage the natural world? Can we assume that we have the ability to manage the natural world? Does it still assume that the planet is a natural resource for use by humans? Does it still assume that humans are morally superior to all other living things?

Why Assume Humans are morally superior to all other species?

Some might say that only members of the species Homo sapiens deserve moral consideration. But how can membership of a particular species be a criterion for moral consideration? Richard Ryder coined the term *"speciesism"*, by analogy with racism and sexism. They all wrongly refuse moral status to certain others simply on the basis of some morally arbitrary distinction. But why should moral status be restricted to only one species? And if so, which species?

It might be argued that a species (or race, or sex) deserve moral status because they possess some unique characteristic. No unique characteristic has been identified that can justify racism. So, racism is morally wrong. But can advocates of anthropocentric ethics identify a qualifying characteristic that justifies speciesism? If we want to say that **ALL** humans and **ONLY** humans deserve moral status then we would have to identify some qualifying characteristic that **ALL** and **ONLY** humans possess.

Is there a unique qualifying property that ONLY humans possess?

Various properties have been suggested. Only humans are rational; only humans can choose to act morally; only humans can use language to discuss moral concepts. So, only humans belong to the 'moral community' of beings that deserve moral consideration. But every qualifying property that has been proposed so far has been shown to be present in other species. It is increasingly widely accepted that many non-human species have some kind of ability to *think*. They can solve problems, use tools, display self-awareness, communicate with each other, and even deceive each other. These are all properties that were at some time thought to be uniquely human, but are no longer considered unique to our species.

Is there a unique qualifying property that ALL humans possess?

Many humans are not rational, nor moral agents, nor language-users. For example, small children, or adults with severe cognitive disabilities, such as Alzheimer's disease, or persons in a coma. As they do not possess the qualifying property, should they be excluded from moral consideration? If so, it could be argued that we can then use them merely as means to achieve our own ends. For example by eating them, hunting them for sport, or performing experiments on them without their consent.

If I could talk, I would argue that treating infants and cognitively disabled adults in the same way that we currently treat non-human animals is an absurd conclusion – oh wait, I can't reason either.

Reductio ad Absurdum

No one is seriously suggesting that we should use babies in laboratory experiments. This is a type of argument that tries to show a statement is false by showing that *if* it was true it would imply an *absurd consequence*, or reduce to an absurdity (*reductio ad absurdum*).

If a claim seems to lead us into an absurd consequence, we have three options:

Bite the bullet and accept the conclusion. But, no moral philosophers have accepted that it would be permissible to use babies in laboratory experiments.

Deny the implication. But, the claim that only beings that possess some qualifying property deserve moral consideration clearly implies that beings that do not possess that property do not deserve moral consideration.

Reject the claim. For all properties suggested so far, it seems that we must reject the claim that only beings possessing that property have moral status.

If we want to draw a dividing line between entities that have moral status and those that do not, then it is important to justify that dividing line. If we arbitrarily assert that all and only humans deserve moral consideration then a racist could equally well assert that only members of one race deserve moral consideration. So, advocates of anthropocentric ethics must find a justification for discriminating between species that cannot be used by racists to justify racism, or sexists to justify sexism, and so on for any other kind of morally arbitrary discrimination. So far however, all attempts to restrict moral status based on some qualifying property have either failed to include all humans, or have implied that we should include at least some non-human beings.

So, anthropocentric ethics may be concerned only with humans. But many environmental problems are harmful to humans. So, anthropocentric ethics can justify stricter environmental policies than those we have today

Yes, but no one has yet provided a convincing argument for restricting moral status to humans. Many think that anthropocentrism itself is the problem. They argue that the scope of moral status should be extended beyond humans

ANIMAL ETHICS

Several philosophers have argued that moral status should be extended to include non-human animals. They argue that causing harm to a non-human animal is morally wrong in itself. It is not enough to say that we are indirectly harming other humans by depleting resources, for example, or depriving them of a source of beauty. Some philosophers still want to restrict moral consideration to humans. But, they have not yet provided a convincing argument to justify excluding non-human animals without also excluding some humans. There is now widespread agreement that non-human animals have at least some kind of moral status. There are right and wrong ways of treating them. However, there is still disagreement about exactly what we can do.

Animal ethics says that non-human animals deserve moral consideration. We should consider the effects of our actions on their interests when making decisions. Animal ethics and environmental ethics are often seen as distinct topics in moral philosophy. However, they are connected. What we do to the environment also affects its non-human inhabitants as well as ourselves. So, when making decisions about actions that might affect the environment, we should consider how they might affect non-human animals. For example, clearing a forest might be beneficial to humans. But, we must also consider the welfare of any non-human animals that might be affected.

Non-human animals are part of the natural world and are affected by what humans do to our mutual environment.

There are various arguments for extending moral status to non-human animals. Some argue that some non-human animals merit moral consideration because we find them beautiful or charismatic.

Many arguments however, are based on the possession of interests. Humans merit moral consideration because they have interests that can be harmed or advanced. But, many non-human animals have interests that can be harmed or advanced. So, if we want to be consistent and avoid moral arbitrariness, then we should accept that non-human animals have moral status.

Animal Liberation

Peter Singer, in *Animal Liberation* (1975), began the current debate on the relative moral status of human and non-human animals. He rejected the view that we can treat non-human animals in any way we want. Non-human animals are not mere automata (as Descartes had suggested) they are **sentient**. That is they have the capacity to feel pleasure and pain. Singer argues that moral status should be extended to all beings possessing sentience. So, when making decisions we should give equal consideration to all sentient beings.

Singer argued that non-human animals are sentient beings that are capable of suffering. Beings that are capable of suffering deserve moral consideration. Ignoring the suffering of non-human animals simply because they are not human would be **speciesism**. So, the interests of sentient non-human animals should merit moral consideration.

43

Utilitarianism

Singer's ethical approach is ***utilitarianism***, which aims to maximize 'utility', happiness or well-being. Utilitarianism is a ***consequentialist*** theory. It is concerned with the consequences of actions. Actions are not 'right' or 'wrong' in themselves. What matters is the balance of good or bad consequences that they produce. We therefore have moral obligations to produce as many good consequences and as few bad consequences as we can.

Jeremy Bentham (1748-1832), the founder of utilitarianism argued that pleasure is the only intrinsically good value in the world and pain is the only thing that is intrinsically bad. So, we have moral obligations to bring about as much happiness, and to reduce suffering as far as we possibly can.

The greatest happiness of the greatest number is the foundation of morals and legislation

Pleasure and Pain

Bentham was one of the first to argue that non-human animals deserve moral consideration. If pleasure and pain are the only intrinsically good and bad things then the criterion for moral status should be the ability to suffer.

The question is not, Can they reason? nor, Can they talk? but, Can they suffer?

Singer developed Bentham's argument further. Utilitarianism is concerned with the balance of pleasure and pain. All sentient beings can feel pleasure and pain. So, the interests of all sentient beings affected by an action should be taken into account in assessing the rightness or wrongness of that action. It is the balance of pleasure and pain that matters, not the individual beings that experience that pleasure or pain. So, we should aim to satisfy the interests in avoiding suffering of as many sentient beings as we can.

Taking into account the suffering of only one species, Homo sapiens, would be speciesism, according to Singer. He considered the animal liberation movement as comparable to other kinds of liberation movements. Nevertheless, Singer's principle of equal consideration of interests need not mean treating all sentient beings equally. Pigs have no interest in voting as they cannot participate in democracy. So, denying pigs the right to vote would not be wrong. But, pigs do have an interest in avoiding suffering. So, ignoring this interest would be wrong.

However, many current practices ignore the suffering of non-human animals. Singer condemns most forms of exploitation of non-human animals, such as hunting, keeping them in zoos, and experimenting on them. For example, the benefits to humans do not outweigh the suffering caused to non-human animals by many experiments, such as testing cosmetics.

Singer's principle might allow humans to eat non-humans, however. Killing a non-human animal painlessly would show consideration for its interest in avoiding suffering. Some species may have sufficient self-consciousness to be capable of having an interest in their future. So, we would have to respect that interest. But, if we can be sure that a being does not have self-consciousness, and if we kill that being painlessly, and if we replace that being with a similar being living a similar life, then we will not reduce the total amount of good in the world. And utilitarianism is concerned only with total amounts of good.

Utilitarianism allows animals to be reared for food provided they are not self-conscious, they live good lives, and they are killed painlessly

But, can these conditions can be met? They are certainly not being met now

Utilitarianism might condemn many current environmental practices. But critics argue that it cannot provide an adequate environmental ethic. It might permit the sacrifice of the interests of individuals for the sake of greater satisfaction of interests for others. Utilitarianism might even allow practices such as hunting, or killing elephants for their ivory. Singer condemns such practices Nevertheless, it might be argued that they produce considerable satisfaction of interests for some humans, and that this outweighs the suffering of the non-human animals involved. Moreover, utilitarianism is not concerned with non-sentient entities, such as plants, rivers, mountains, or landscapes unless these have instrumental value to sentient beings. But these are all objects of moral concern to environmentalists.

Animal Rights

Tom Regan, in *The Case for Animal Rights* (1983) argues that non-human animals have moral rights. He argues that moral status should be extended to all "*subjects-of-a-life*". We all have our own unique life stories and we are the subjects of those stories.

Subjects-of-a-life have beliefs and desires; perception, memory, and a sense of the future, including their own future; an emotional life together with feelings of pleasure and pain; preference- and welfare-interests; the ability to initiate action in pursuit of their desires and goals; a psychological identity over time; and an individual welfare in the sense that their experiential life fares well or ill for them

Deontological Ethics (Rights)

Regan's view is a *deontological* ethical theory (from the Greek word δέον, deon, "duty" or "obligation"). Deontological theories are concerned with whether an action is right or wrong in itself regardless of its consequences. Observing certain moral rules or duties, such as "do not kill", "do not lie", is intrinsically right and violating them intrinsically wrong.

Immanuel Kant (1724 – 1804) founded modern deontological ethics. He argued that morality is based on absolute unconditional requirements, or *categorical imperatives*.

A *hypothetical* imperative might say –

> *IF* you want to be trusted you should keep your promises

A *categorical* imperative would simply state

> Keep your promises!

The Categorical Imperative

Kant expressed the fundamental categorical imperative in different ways, one of which requires respect for persons. Persons cannot be used *merely* as a means to an end. Persons have ends of their own which deserve moral respect. Persons can be used *with* their consent, as when an employee voluntarily consents to be used as a means to the ends of the employer. But, slavery is not acceptable. Slavery uses persons *merely* as a means to the ends of others.

Act in such a way that you treat humanity, whether in your own person or in the person of any other, never merely as a means to an end, but always at the same time as an end.

Ms Jones, send in a scapegoat

The categorical imperative implies that persons have moral **rights** to be treated in certain ways and other persons have moral **duties** to respect those rights. Deontologists believe that all humans have moral rights to be treated respectfully because all humans have intrinsic value.

Subjects of a Life

Kant believed that all humans have intrinsic value because they are rational. But infants and cognitively disabled adults are not rational. Nevertheless, most deontologists would still wish to say that infants and cognitively disabled adults have rights. Regan solves this problem by arguing that the only property that has intrinsic value and which all humans possess is to be a "subject-of-a-life". We each have a unique life story and we are the subjects of that life story. Beings that are subjects-of-a-life have intrinsic value, and thus rights. But many species are subjects-of-a-life. So, Regan argues, if we believe that infants and severely cognitively disabled adults deserve rights then we must believe that many other species also deserve rights.

Regan's view, unlike Singer's, would not permit experiments on individuals with intrinsic value, regardless of any greater good that might arise for others. It would also rule out many other practices, such as hunting. Utilitarianism might allow the interests of individuals to be overridden for the greater good of others. But, for deontologists, it is not interests that matter but the beings that possess those interests. Regan's rights-based approach prohibits using individuals merely as means no matter how great the satisfaction of interests for others it may produce. We have a moral duty not to use subjects-of-a-life merely as a means.

Thus any practice that fails to respect the rights of those animals who have them, e.g. eating animals, hunting animals, experimenting on animals, using animals for entertainment, is wrong, irrespective of human need, context, or culture.

The animal rights view would condemn many current practices. We have a duty not to harm beings that are subjects-of-a-life. But, hunting and experimenting on non-human animals violate the rights of intrinsically valuable beings. So, such actions are intrinsically wrong, regardless of whatever consequences may arise from them. The animal rights approach requires radical changes to the way we currently treat non-human animals. Utilitarianism might permit non-human animals to be reared for food. But, no matter how humanely they are reared and how painlessly they are killed, we are using them merely as a means to our own ends and not as ends in themselves. So, it is morally wrong to raise animals for food. Likewise for animal experimentation, hunting and so on.

...animals are treated routinely, systematically as if their value were reducible to their usefulness to others, they are routinely, systematically treated with a lack of respect, and thus are their rights routinely, systematically violated ...

Virtue Ethics

The third major tradition in western moral philosophy is **virtue ethics**. Virtue ethics is based on persons rather than actions. Utilitarianism and deontological ethics try to find rules to tell us what to do. Following those rules might be considered 'virtuous'. But virtue ethics claims that the virtues come first. Rules, if any, should be derived from the virtues. Virtue ethics asks us to think about what sort of person *to be*, rather than what is the right thing *to do*.

Virtues are the character traits and behaviours that persons need to live well

A virtuous person is someone who possesses the relevant virtues and acts in accordance with them.

The right thing to do is what a virtuous person would do in the circumstances.

Aristotle (384 – 322 BC) believed that the highest human good is εὐδαιμονία (eudaimonia), happiness, well-being, or living well. It is now usually translated as flourishing, or achieving our potential. Flourishing involves cultivating the virtues and living in accordance with them.

55

Virtue ethics ask us to think about what sort of person we want to be. If we want to be good persons, what character traits should we develop? What behaviours should parents teach their children if they want them to grow up to be good persons? People are often praised or blamed for their characters traits and behaviours. Virtue ethics requires us to be virtuous persons. That is to develop virtuous character traits and behaviours. Virtuous persons abhor the corresponding vices. So, virtuous persons act in accordance with their virtues and do not act in accordance with vices.

People are praised for *virtuous* character traits, such as benevolence, kindness, generosity, courage ...

People are blamed for *vicious* character traits, such as selfishness, cruelty, spitefulness, cowardice ...

Virtue ethics does not give us rules to follow. Virtuous persons act in accordance with their virtues. But, what if we have not developed the relevant virtues and are not sure what we should do? Virtue ethics tells us that we should aim to do whatever a virtuous person would do in the circumstances.

So, how would a virtuous person treat non-human animals?

One suggested answer is "with compassion". Virtue ethicists commonly recognize compassion as a virtue. Non-human animals are relatively powerless compared to humans. Few people would consider harming powerless beings and displaying indifference to their suffering to be an expression of compassion. So, at the very least a virtuous person would refrain from causing gratuitous suffering to non-human animals.

Critics say however, that virtue ethics is too vague to provide guidance for our actions. It is not always clear what a virtuous person would do. Moreover, there is no general agreement on what the virtues are. Different cultures may regard different characteristics as virtuous. Attempts to devise lists of virtues and vices have so far proved contentious. One person's vice could be another person's virtue.

Hunting involves risk to the hunter. So, it displays the virtue of courage.

Virtue ethicists can respond that whether or not an action is virtuous depends on its motives. It must be done for the right reasons. For example, the virtue of courage involves taking risks for good reasons. Taking risks for no good reason is recklessness. Hunting involving risks undertaken to enjoy the sadistic pleasure of causing suffering would be a vice. Hunting involving risks undertaken as the only way to feed a starving family could be a virtue. However, a virtuous person would regret, not enjoy, the necessity.

Virtue ethics then, like utilitarianism and deontological ethics, would condemn most current practices. Hunting, factory farming and animal experimentation are all inimical to the flourishing of the non-human animals involved. The three ethical approaches differ theoretically. Utilitarianism and deontological ethics try to devise general rules applicable to all situations. Virtue ethics does not try to devise universal rules but relies on the exercise of judgement in particular situations. Nevertheless, despite their theoretical differences, the three approaches tend to converge towards similar practical implications for our current treatment of non-human animals.

Questions for animal ethics
What if human and non-human interests conflict?

If human and non-human animals should be treated with equal moral consideration then how do we resolve conflicts of interests? Tom Regan discusses this question. Suppose a lifeboat can support only four lives, but it contains five passengers, four humans and a dog. Either all will die, or one can be thrown overboard. But, if they all have rights, then which should it be?

We drew lots. You lost.

Regan argues, the dog can be thrown overboard because loss of life is a much greater harm to a human than to a dog. But critics might say that as an experiencing subject-of-a-life, a dog's desires and goals are as important to the dog as a human's are to the human. If we want to avoid being arbitrary, by what objective standard can we decide which experiences of which subjects-of-a-life are more important?

Utilitarians on a sinking lifeboat might decide which to throw overboard by estimating utilities, and maximising happiness, or minimizing suffering. But, suppose whoever is chosen will be killed quickly and painlessly. Suppose also that no one else is affected. All family and friends sank with the ship. No suffering is involved. So, the decision must minimize loss of happiness. Dogs are easily pleased. So, should the least happy human be thrown overboard?

Bentham's utilitarianism aims to maximize pleasure and minimize suffering. But, different individuals have different interests. Singer's version of utilitarianism aims to maximize the satisfaction of whatever interests different individuals prefer. Humans have more preferences than dogs. So, Singer, like Regan, would throw the dog overboard.

Nevertheless, it might be argued that babies and severely cognitively disabled adults do not have many preferences. So, how would **preference utilitarianism** resolve conflicts between the interests of babies or cognitively disabled adults and those of non-human animals?

Virtue ethics suggests applying judgement to particular cases rather than following general rules. Conflicts between human and non-human interests are resolved by appeal to the virtues. A virtuous person might feel compassion for the suffering of all sentient beings. But, if forced to make a choice, compassion for fellow humans might override compassion for non-human animals.

Many people would agree that virtuous humans would feel more compassion for other humans than for other species, just as they would feel more compassion for their own families than for complete strangers. But this is unavoidably speciesist. So, how can virtue ethics avoid anthropocentrism?

Moreover, virtue ethics allows us to treat different species (or strangers) differently. But it does not tell us precisely how we can treat them. We cannot do anything we want to strangers to benefit our own families. Similarly, we cannot do anything we want to other species. But, what precisely can we do?

Does animal ethics conflict with environmentalism?

If we have obligations to alleviate the suffering of non-human animals then do we have obligations to prevent predators from killing their prey? If non-human animals have rights, then do we have obligations to prevent predators from violating the rights of their prey? This seems an absurd conclusion to many people. Moreover, how could such a policy be implemented?

Moreover, many environmentalists are concerned with the preservation of natural habitats and processes. But, they argue, the predator-prey relationship is an essential aspect of healthy ecosystems. So, how can we both protect prey from predators and preserve natural habitats?

How would we protect species and ecosystems?

Many environmentalists are concerned not about individual beings, but about whole species and ecosystems. However, concern for the whole may sometimes conflict with the interests of individuals. For example, some invasive species may damage ecosystems or local biodiversity. If only individual beings deserve moral consideration then culling cannot be justified. But, how would we maintain biodiversity and healthy ecosystems?

How would we protect endangered species?

If individuals are all that matter then the last surviving panda deserves no more moral consideration than a stray cat. But, many environmentalists would argue that more consideration is owed to endangered species.

I have the same rights as you. I can suffer as much as you can. I could flourish as well as you can!

Tell me more about life on the endangered list.

So, animal ethics does have profound implications for environmental ethics. Environmental policy decisions should take into account both human and non-human animals. A healthy environment is essential for the well-being of the non-human as well as human animals that it contains.

Nevertheless, concern for individual animals might conflict with concerns for whole species and ecosystems. Animal ethics would give priority to individual animals over environmental issues. So, perhaps the scope of moral status should be extended further.

BIOCENTRIC ETHICS

Suppose the last man was also the last sentient being. Would he be wrong to destroy the rest of the world? No sentient beings would be harmed. So, according to animal-centred ethics the last man has done nothing wrong. But, many people still feel intuitively that the last man has done something wrong. So, some environmental philosophers believe that the scope of moral status should be extended to include all living organisms, regardless of whether or not those organisms are sentient.

Biocentric (life-centred) ethics extends moral status to all living things in nature. All living organisms have intrinsic value, regardless of whether or not they are useful to humans, or even to sentient non-human animals.

Reverence for Life

Albert Schweitzer (1875 – 1965) advocated *"reverence for Life"*. All living things have a "will to live" and humans should not interfere with this will.

Ethics is nothing other than Reverence for Life. Reverence for Life affords me my fundamental principle of morality, namely, that good consists in maintaining, assisting and enhancing life, and to destroy, to harm or to hinder life is evil

But, it might be argued that although it is clear that living organisms struggle for survival, it is not clear that they have a will to live. A will to live would require some kind of conscious experience. But many organisms do not have any obvious kind of consciousness. So, they would not merit moral status.

Respect for Nature

Paul Taylor, in *Respect for Nature* (1986), argued that consciousness is not necessary for moral status. Regardless of whether they are conscious or not, all living things strive towards a good of their own. If they have a good of their own they deserve moral respect. Taylor argues that ethical theories have three components: a belief system, a moral attitude, and a set of moral rules and standards. For example, human ethics is based on equal respect for persons.

We believe that we are all *persons*: subjective centres of consciousness able to choose our own values and direct our own lives.

I believe I deserve respect as a person. So, it is reasonable to adopt a moral attitude of respect for all other persons and to expect all other persons to have the same moral attitude.

So, we follow whatever moral rules and standards best express this attitude of equal *respect for persons*.

Taylor argues that an environmental ethic would similarly comprise three components: a belief system, a moral attitude, and a set of moral rules. He argues that *a **biocentric outlook on Nature*** would be a reasonable belief system. If we accept the biocentric belief system then we will see that the only appropriate moral attitude would be ***respect for nature***. Respect for nature would be best expressed by an ethical system that has come to be known as ***biocentric egalitarianism***.

Taylor proposes four core beliefs of the biocentric outlook on nature.

Humans are members of the Earths Community of Life

All living things are related to one another in an order of interdependence

Each organism is a teleological centre of life

Humans are not superior to other forms of life

Humans are members of "Earth's Community of Life"

Humans are an integral part of the natural order of the Earth's biosphere. Taylor argues that all species, including humans, share a common relationship to the Earth. All have similar biological requirements for survival and well-being. All have a good of their own. All need the freedom to promote or protect that good in accordance with their nature. Humans are a recent arrival on the planet. Its order of life existed for billions of years before us. Humans depend upon the soundness and good health of the Earth's biosphere, but its soundness and good health is not dependent upon humans.

All living things are related to one another in an order of interdependence.

The Earth's biosphere is a complex but unified web of interconnected organisms. Organisms are intricately connected to each other in relationships such as food chains, predator-prey relations and plant succession in forests. These relationships form self-regulating energy-recycling mechanisms that preserve the equilibrium of the whole. The survival and the well-being of each living thing depends on the stability of this ecological equilibrium.

Taylor forestalls the objection that this view might imply that the good of the whole is more important than the good of individuals. He emphasizes that only individual living organisms are morally significant. Ecosystems are not morally significant themselves except in so far as they provide the conditions for realizing the good of individual living organisms. So, "respect for nature" really means respect for the individual living things in nature, not for nature itself.

Each organism is a "teleological centre of life".

Each individual organism pursues its own good in its own way. Each individual organism, including humans, is a *"teleological (goal-oriented) centre of life"*. It's internal functioning and external activities are all goal-oriented. They tend to maintain the organism's existence and to perform its biological operations.

Taylor forestalls the charge of **anthropomorphism**[*], the projection of human thoughts and feelings onto non-human entities. A teleological centre of life is a unified system of organized activity, that may or may not be conscious, but that has a good of its own that it tends to promote. A stone does not have a good of its own that we can benefit or harm. But, a tree, does have a good of its own. A tree might not consciously desire water, sunlight and nutrition, but these are all good for its biological flourishing.

[*] *Cartoonists are exempt*

Humans are not superior to other forms of life.

Taylor rejects anthropocentric arguments that humans are morally superior to all other species. No one has yet found a property that *all* and *only* humans possess that would qualify humans for moral status. Furthermore, if we accept the first three core beliefs of the biocentric outlook, if we see ourselves as integral parts of the Earth's community of life, having a deep kinship, and sharing many common characteristics with all other living things each, like us, pursuing their own good, then we will see that the idea of human superiority is unreasonable. No bias of one species over another is acceptable.

Respect for nature is the only appropriate attitude.

If we accept the core beliefs of the biocentric outlook on nature, Taylor argues, we would see that respect for nature is the only appropriate moral attitude. There is no good reason to say that some humans are superior to others within human society. If we see all humans as equal persons, equal centres of conscious life, then we will see that the only appropriate attitude is to treat all persons with equal moral respect. Similarly, there is no good reason to say that some species are superior to others within the community of life. If we see all living organisms as equal teleological centres of life then we will see that the only appropriate attitude is to treat all living things with equal moral respect.

What does Taylor mean by saying that a living thing has 'a good of its own'?

An entity has a 'good of its own' if we can say that some things can be good or bad for that entity without reference to any other entity.

For example, it is generally accepted that humans have a good of their own. We can say that something is good or bad for a human without referring to anyone else. Machines do not have a good of their own. We would not say that something is good or bad for a machine. We can only say that something is good or bad for those who use the machine as a means to their own ends.

An entity does not have to be conscious to have a good of its own. Taylor claims that the good for an individual organism is the full development of its biological powers, whether or not it is conscious. He explains this by distinguishing between **having an interest** in something, and something **being in our interest.** We have a *subjective* interest in what we *believe* might be good for us. But, we often make mistakes in our subjective values. If something *in fact* contributes to our true good then *it is in* our *objective* interest.

I do not **have a subjective interest** in eating my greens

But, eating your greens is **in your objective interest**

Some things clearly are objectively good or bad for us, regardless of what we subjectively believe. Similarly, some things are objectively good or bad for non-human animals and plants. It is not relevant whether or not they possess sufficient consciousness to have subjective interests. But, it is in their objective interests to achieve full development of their biological potential. And these objective interests can be benefited or harmed by our actions.

All entities that have a good of their own have "inherent worth". Taylor's use of the term 'inherent worth' appears to suggest objective intrinsic value. That is, entities with 'inherent worth' have value in themselves for their own sake regardless of their usefulness or subjective value to others. Moreover, they have this value regardless of whether or not they are conscious. Taylor argues that if we believe that we ourselves have inherent worth because we have a good of our own, then it is reasonable to accept that all other entities that have a good of their own have inherent worth. And if we believe we deserve moral respect ourselves as beings with inherent worth then it is reasonable to adopt an attitude of respect to all other beings we believe to have inherent worth.

Their value of worth does not depend on their being valued for their usefulness in furthering human ends

Biocentric egalitarianism is the appropriate ethical system.

If we adopt an attitude of respect for living things then, Taylor argues, this respect would be best expressed by an ethical system that takes equal account of the interests of all living organisms. This ethical view is now known as *biocentric egalitarianism*.

Taylor does not claim that all living things have rights. In his view rights are applicable only to beings that are capable of making moral judgements. So, we do not have duties to non-human living organisms because they have rights. But, if we have an attitude of respect for nature then we would accept certain *moral duties* towards all living organisms that have a good of their own.

A duty not to cause harm

A duty not to interfere

A duty not to deceive

GAME BIRD
BATTERY CAGES

And a duty to make amends for violating any of these three duties

If we have multiple duties, there is always a risk of conflicts of duties. Moreover, almost everything humans do involves some harm to other living organisms, eating, providing clothing and shelter and so on. So, Taylor also provides a set of principles to resolve these unavoidable conflicts of interests.

Conflict Resolution Principles

Humans can defend themselves against harmful organisms

Humans cannot harm non-humans to satisfy trivial interests

Humans can harm non-humans to satisfy important interests, but must minimize any wrong done

Humans must make restitution for any wrong done

So, we cannot harm non-human organisms for trivial reasons, such as hunting for pleasure or making ornaments from body parts. We can harm non-human organisms for important reasons, such as growing crops, and killing weeds if necessary, in order to feed ourselves. For example, Taylor argues that respect for nature supports vegetarianism. Raising crops to feed animals then eating those animals is more destructive than raising crops to feed ourselves directly.

Questions for biocentric ethics.

Is "being alive" a sufficient condition for possessing moral status?

It might be argued that even if a plant has an objective good of its own, if the plant does not consciously care about its own good, then why should we?

The Golden Rule says that we should treat others as we would wish to be treated. If I was a tree I wouldn't care what happens to me. So, I don't care what happens to the tree.

But, this is precisely the view that Taylor argued against. That was why he distinguished *having an interest* from something *being in our interest*. We do not have to try to imagine what (if any) subjective interests something might have, but we can still care about what is in its objective interests.

Do we have moral obligations to promote objective interests?

It might be argued that we do not have moral obligations to the objective good of other entities, but only to their welfare, how well their lives are going from their point of view. But, entities without consciousness do not have a point of view. So, we do not have moral obligations to entities without consciousness.

In response, biocentric ethicists might reject the claim that we have moral obligations *only* to beings with a point of view. Taylor acknowledges that he does not prove that we *must* accept moral obligations to promote the objective good of other entities. He argues only that if we accept the biocentric outlook then we would see that equal respect for all living things was the most appropriate attitude. So, this objection does not refute Taylor's argument, though the response may make it seem less persuasive.

Is equal respect for all living things the most appropriate attitude?

It might be argued that we could accept the first three elements of the biocentric outlook, but reject the fourth, the denial of human superiority. We might accept the claim that all living things have **equal moral status**. But, it might be argued that this is not the same as **equal moral significance**.

Biocentrists might respond that many philosophers believe the concept of moral hierarchy is dubious. Moreover, if the moral significance of plants is so low that we can destroy them, why bother accepting they have moral status?

Is biocentric ethics too individualistic?

Like anthropocentric and animal-centred ethics, biocentric ethics is concerned with individuals. So, it is difficult to account for obligations to species and ecosystems. The moral significance of individual living entities might conflict with attempts to preserve species or to maintain ecosystems. For example, it would not justify eradicating invasive species in order to maintain biodiversity.

In response, biocentric ethicists could argue that species and ecosystems are not important in themselves, but only for the flourishing of the individuals that comprise them. But, if species and ecosystems are important only for the flourishing of individuals, then how do we balance moral concern for some individuals against others within those species and ecosystems? For example, how do we balance respect for individuals belonging to native species against respect for those belonging to invasive species.

ECOCENTRIC ETHICS

Ecocentric (*ecology-centred*) philosophies devise arguments based on ecology. Ecology is the study of the interactions of living organisms with each other and with their environment. Ecology is *holistic*. It is concerned with such things as species and ecosystems as a whole. Ecosystems are regions in which various living organisms interact in mutually beneficial ways with each other and with their non-living environment, for example, forests, lakes and deserts. Ecocentric philosophies consider species and ecosystems to be more than merely the sum of the individuals that belong to them.

Ecocentric ethics is holistic rather than individualistic. It extends the scope of moral status to include ecological wholes and away from individual plants and animals. Whole species or whole ecosystems possess moral status, independently of the individuals that make up the whole system.

Holism

Traditional theories are analytical. They analyse things into parts and try to understand the whole from what they understand of the parts. Holistic theories try to understand the whole, then to understand the parts from what they understand of the whole. Ecological holists try to understand the interconnections between all elements of ecosystems. They think in terms of the complex web of the natural environment rather than in terms of individuals.

The Land Ethic

Aldo Leopold's *A Sand Country Almanac* (1949) is the main influence on holistic ethics. Leopold advocated a "***land ethic***" that deals with the relations between humans and the land they inhabit. He believed that ethics progressed from dealing with relations between individuals to dealing with relations between the individual and society. Individuals learn to cooperate as members of an interdependent community. But, now, there is a need for a further progression, an ethics dealing with relations between humans and the land.

The land ethic simply enlarges the boundaries of the community to include soils, waters, plants, and animals, or collectively: the land

A land ethic changes the role of Homo sapiens from conqueror of the land-community to plain member and citizen of it

A ***biota*** is the collection of organisms in a region, and the ***biotic community*** is the biota and their interrelationships. The land ethic implies respect not only for individual organisms, but also for the biotic community that they comprise. Respect for the biotic community implies that we would stop treating the land merely as an economic resource.

Leopold argued that conservation requires an "**ecological conscience**", a sense of individual responsibility for the health of the land. Contemporary conservation treated land as a resource and was based on economic self-interest. Some individuals might ignore conservation principles that are beneficial to the community and accept only those that are in their own individual self-interest. But many people already do accept obligations over and above self-interest within communities. So, Leopold argues, if conservation is to be successful we need a similar sense of communal obligations towards the land.

Obligations have no meaning without conscience, and the problem we face is the extension of the social conscience from people to land

If we are to develop an ecological conscience then, Leopold suggests, we would be better of viewing land not as an economic resource but as a **land pyramid**. The pyramid comprises successive layers, each dependent on those below it. The bottom layer of the pyramid is the soil. A plant layer rests on the soil, an insect layer rests on the plant layer, and so on through successive layers to the top predators at the apex. Moreover, essential circuits of energy flow through the successive layers of the pyramid. The land pyramid does change over time. But, evolutionary changes are usually slow and local. Humans have introduced changes that are of "unprecedented violence, rapidity, and scope".

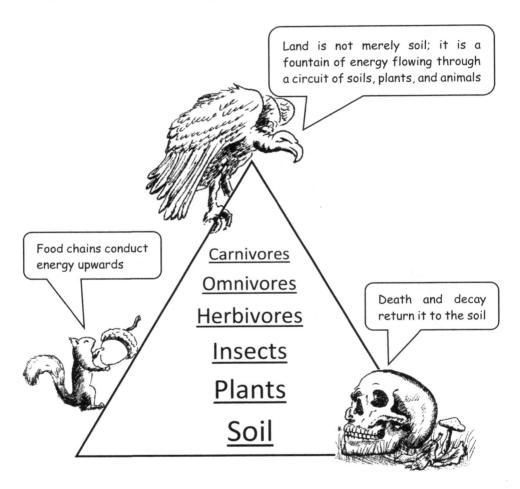

The health of the land pyramid is its capacity to renew itself following changes. **Conservation** is our attempt to preserve this capacity for self-renewal. Relationships within the land pyramid are too complex and not all of economic value. So, conservation efforts based on economic self-interest and that treat land as soil are unlikely to be successful. Successful conservation requires a view of the land as a biota, the development of an ecological conscience and a land ethic. So, preserving the health of the land then, is not merely a matter of economic expedience, but also of ethical right and wrong.

A thing is right when it tends to preserve the integrity, stability, and beauty of the biotic community. It is wrong when it tends otherwise

The is/ought gap

Leopold moves from **descriptive** statements about **how the world is** to **prescriptive** statements about **how the world ought to be**. Even if the land pyramid describes how the world is, why should we accept what the land ethic tells us we ought to do?

Many philosophers accept **Hume's law**, also known as the **"is/ought gap"**, which claims that we cannot use facts about how the world **is** to derive conclusions about how the world **ought** to be. We cannot use facts to derive values.

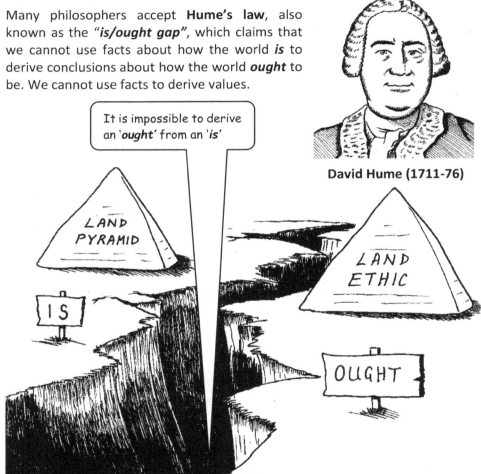

It is impossible to derive an '**ought**' from an '**is**'

David Hume (1711-76)

LAND PYRAMID

LAND ETHIC

IS

OUGHT

Many philosophers therefore, can argue that Leopold's argument does not justify the Land Ethic. Some further theoretical justification is required.

Facts and Values

Some philosophers claim that facts and values are entirely distinct things. Facts can tell us nothing at all about values. Others argue that facts and values are not so easy to separate. However, all accept the is/ought gap as a matter of logic. A logically valid conclusion cannot contain anything that is not in the premises. So, if there is an 'ought' in the conclusion, there must be an 'ought' (either explicitly or at least implicitly) somewhere in the premises.

So, values cannot be derived solely from facts. But, values can be derived from other values combined with facts. That is, an "ought" statement can be derived from an "is" statement combined with another "ought" statement. It is sometimes possible to *"**bridge the is/ought gap**"*. That is, construct an argument with an 'ought' in the conclusion that is logically valid. If you accept the premises then the conclusion does logically follow from those premises.

For example:-

> We **ought** to avoid causing gratuitous suffering. It **is a fact** that non-human animals can suffer. So, we **ought** to avoid causing gratuitous suffering to non-human animals.

Objective Intrinsic Value

Holmes Rolston III provides another argument to bridge the is/ought gap. He argues that individual living organisms and holistic entities, such as species, ecosystems and the biosphere, have ***objective intrinsic value***. It is not enough to say that organisms, species or ecosystems have *instrumental value* as resources for humans, nor is it enough to say that they have some *subjective intrinsic value* that human feelings may project onto them. He cites various example that appear to support his view. For example, certain unscrupulous butterfly collectors may destroy rare butterfly species in order to increase the economic value of the specimens they have already collected. Many people would agree that this seems morally wrong, yet it is difficult to say why solely in terms of human-centred instrumental or subjective values.

So, facts about how the world is can sometimes tell us something about how the world ought to be. For example, we accept that we ought not to cause gratuitous suffering. We now generally recognize as a fact that non-human animals can suffer. So, we now generally accept that we ought not to cause gratuitous suffering to non-human animals. In Rolston's terms, we recognize that non-human animals have intrinsic value and deserve moral consideration.

Rolston argues furthermore, that all living organisms have intrinsic value. Individual living organisms have a good of their own. Things can go better or worse for them. A living organisms defend its own good. So, for an organism there is the way the world is, and a way the world ought to be. There seems no good reason, he claims, why organisms with a good of their own are not morally significant. So, living organisms have objective intrinsic value.

This is how the world is, but it is not how it ought to be

Moreover, Rolston argues, objective intrinsic value permeates the entire biotic community. He argues that individual organisms do not exist in isolation, but are part of a biotic web of other organisms and ecosystems. Their existence is made possible by the biotic web, and they contribute to the web. Nor can organisms be valued in isolation. If individual organisms have value then the species that makes possible the existence of those individuals must have value.

+

If, in this world of uncertain moral convictions, it makes any sense to claim that one ought not to kill individuals, without justification, it makes more sense to claim that one ought not to superkill the species, without superjustification

If species have value then the ecosystems that make possible the diversity of species must have value. The evolutionary processes that make possible the existence of ecosystems must have value. The biotic sphere that makes possible evolutionary processes and biodiversity and individual organisms, including humans, must have value.

Moral Sentiments

J. Baird Callicott believes that subjective intrinsic value may be easier to justify than objective intrinsic value. He argues that the land ethic belongs in the tradition of *moral sentiments*. Utilitarianism and deontological ethics attempt to justify ethics using reason. But, some philosophers, including **David Hume** and **Adam Smith**, have argued that ethics is based not on reason, but on *altruistic feelings*, such as benevolence and sympathy. We enjoy the happiness of others and are distressed by the suffering of others. So we approve of actions that benefit others and disapprove of actions that harm others.

There is no spectacle so fair and beautiful as a noble and generous action; nor any which gives us more abhorrence than one that is cruel and treacherous

How selfish soever man may be supposed, there are evidently some principles in his nature, which interest him in the fortunes of others, and render their happiness necessary to him, though he derives nothing from it, except the pleasure of seeing it

Adam Smith (1723-90)

Charles Darwin suggested that social animals, such as humans, evolved altruistic feelings in order to cooperate within mutually beneficial societies. Callicott argues that natural selection has thus given humans a strong sense of empathy towards other members of our communities. Affections and sympathies between parents and offspring are common to most mammals. These affections can be extended beyond immediate family members, allowing larger groups to form. Larger groups may be better able to provide for themselves. So, by natural selection, altruistic feelings could spread through a population. Moreover, humans evolved intelligence and language. They could therefore, express their altruistic feelings in codes of ethics. Humans may discuss ethics in terms of reason, but ethical codes are ultimately based on altruistic feelings.

As societies grew larger and more complex so too did systems of ethics. Darwin suggested that as small tribes united into larger communities, individuals recognized that they ought to extend their social sympathies to all members of the larger communities. So, if morality is founded on social sympathies then the scope of morality will extend to the boundaries of the community. Callicott suggests that we have now reached a stage at which many humans accept that we are members of a global community, with a common ethics of universal human rights.

The next stage will be to recognize the significance of the biotic community. Ecological sciences show that plants, animals (human and non-human), soils and waters are all interlocked in one community, one biota.

It would therefore be reasonable to develop sympathy and fellow-feeling for fellow members of our biotic community, and feelings of loyalty towards the community as a whole. So, it is possible to develop a land ethic based on altruistic feelings. Moreover, given our destructive potential, it is necessary.

Questions for ecocentric ethics.

Does it require sacrificing individuals for the good of the whole?

A big problem for ecocentric ethics is how to balance individual interests against those of the community as a whole. The land ethic extends moral status to the community as a whole. So, it could be interpreted as suggesting that only the biotic community has intrinsic value. Individuals have merely instrumental value depending on their contribution to the larger biotic whole. So, this view permits the sacrifice of individuals in order to protect the "integrity, stability, and beauty" of the larger biotic community.

For example, it might permit culling invasive species to protect the holistic good of the community. But, the most destructive species to the biotic community is *Homo sapiens*. So, to be consistent, the land ethic would permit culling humans for the greater good of the biotic community as a whole.

In response, Callicott argues that the charge of *"**environmental fascism**"* assumes that entities deserve moral status because they possess some qualifying property. If the qualifying property of the land ethic is membership of the biotic community then all members of the community would have equal rights and all would be equally subordinate to the greater good of the community. However, Callicott argues that the land ethic is based on ***moral sentiments***. We may have altruistic feelings to the community. But we belong to several layers of successively larger communities. We are firstly members of families, then of local communities, of national communities, of the human community in general, then of the biotic community.

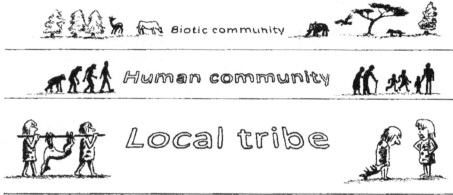

Membership of communities gives us obligations. But obligations to larger communities do not replace those to smaller communities. Obligations to families come before obligations to nations and to the human community in general. So, we may recognize that we are members of the biotic community as well as of the human community, but still place obligations to humans before obligations to the biotic community.

Callicott devised *"second order" principles* to prioritize moral obligations to human communities over obligations to natural communities.

Who decides the priorities of the various community obligations?

If it is left for individuals to decide for themselves then, how do we avoid people giving priority to morally repugnant obligations? For example, racists could claim that they feel a greater sense of obligation towards their own racial 'communities', than to the rest of the human community.

If it is not left for individuals to decide for themselves then some objective standard is required. But, how do we find and agree an objective standard? How should it be enforced?

Moreover, ecocentric ethics was intended to avoid anthropocentrism. But, if obligations to the human community override obligations to the biotic community, then are we back to anthropocentrism?

Are moral sentiments too unreliable?

The moral sentiments tradition avoids specifying precise rules. But, without rules to resolve conflicts between obligations, is it too unreliable? Moreover, our moral attitude would depend on our empathy. If we empathize with the suffering of others we tend not to harm them and may try to benefit them. But, many people feel no empathy for the biotic community. How can people who do not feel any empathy towards non-human entities be persuaded that they should accept moral obligations to the environment?

Should we be "guided by nature"?

John Stuart Mill rejects the view that we should follow nature. He argues that values are found in civilization. The natural world is full of death and suffering. If 'nature' means things as they would be without human intervention then to follow nature would be both *irrational* and *immoral*.

It would be *irrational* because all human actions consist in altering nature, and all useful actions in attempting to improve on nature. It would be *immoral* because natural phenomena cause death, destruction and enormous suffering. Anyone copying those natural phenomena would be seen as "the wickedest of men".

Nearly all the things which men are imprisoned for doing to one another, are nature's every day performances

John Stuart Mill (1806 – 1873)

Rolston agrees that nature is amoral, or even immoral. Nature does not tell us how to behave towards each other. But, it can tell us how to behave towards the natural environment. Nature can be hostile to life, but nature also gave us life. Natural ecological processes made possible the emergence of humans. Natural death and decay recycle resources and make possible new life. We can and ought to resist the harmful aspects of nature, disease and death, cold and hunger. But if we want to maintain a good fit with the natural environment and live efficiently and wisely then, Rolston concludes, we can and ought to follow nature by letting it teach us something of our human role and appropriate character in the natural system as a whole.

Rolston even calls Mill as a witness.

What do we mean by 'nature' anyway?

Mill also points out that the term 'nature' is ambiguous. Sometimes it refers to the entire world, including humans. But, in this sense of the term, we have no choice but to follow nature. Humans are a product of nature. So, everything we do and make would be natural in this sense. So, to say that we should be guided by nature would be superfluous.

However, Mill suggests, the term 'nature' is also used in a second sense to refer to the world as it would be without human interference. In this sense, something is **'natural'** as opposed to **'artificial'**. It is following nature in this second sense of the term that Mill argues would be irrational and immoral.

Mill agreed that nature can be useful. But, it is also often hostile. So, we cannot rely on nature to tell us what we ought to do and we should modify nature, when we can and when it is too our own benefit. Value is found not in nature, according to Mill, but in the artificial world we create against hostile nature.

Some environmentalists accept Mill's distinction between natural and artificial, but argue that nature is nevertheless valuable in itself, because it is irreplaceable, or because it reminds us of our limits and our place in the world. So, they claim, unspoiled nature has value in itself. They are concerned with preserving areas of natural wilderness as distinct from the artificial environment that we inhabit.

Is there a clear distinction between natural and artificial?

There is not much natural wilderness left in the world. Most landscapes are artificial. In northern Europe, environmentalism is often concerned with protecting local rural landscapes. But, these are artificial products of centuries of traditional cultivation. Nevertheless, even artificial landscapes can have significant ecological value. For example, conservationists object to digging up hedgerows. But, hedgerows were planted at some time, and are thus artificial. Nevertheless, they are considered valuable for their historical and traditional associations as well as for their contemporary ecological value.

So, 'natural' seems to be a relative term. Environmentalism can often involve a concern for both natural and artificial aspects of our environment. The problem then is how to balance these concerns.

So, ecocentric ethics gives good reasons to accept that holistic entities, such as species and ecosystems, have value independently of humans, and that they merit moral status

But, it might justify sacrificing individuals, even humans, for the greater holistic good. The more we extend the scope of moral status the more moral conflicts we seem to have to solve. So, where should we draw the line?

WHERE DO WE DRAW THE LINE?

We believe that all humans deserve equal moral status. But, there seems no good reason to restrict the scope of moral status to humans. So, an important question that all attempts to extend traditional moral theories have to answer is how far can we extend the scope of moral status.

Utilitarians draw the line at *sentience*. Sentience is now widely recognized as an important line. It is now generally agreed that causing gratuitous suffering to sentient beings is wrong. But, there is still disagreement about how much non-human sentient beings should count, and about how to resolve conflicts of interests between human and non-human sentient beings.

Plants are not sentient. They do not suffer pain, nor do they possess conscious interests. But, it is reasonable to say that certain things can be in their interests. Things can go better or worse for them. Plants can also possess some intrinsic properties that are said to give humans moral status, such as beauty, or the property of being a complex living thing. So, should we draw the line around all living things?

But, things can go better or worse for ecosystems and the biosphere. It is a matter of debate whether or not ecosystems and the biosphere should be considered as living or non-living things. But, even non-living things can possess aesthetic beauty or be complex systems. For example, rivers, rocks and mountains and entire ecosystems.

Extending traditional moral theories does provide some useful approaches towards dealing with environmental ethical problems. But, there are still many questions to be investigated. Moreover, the further the scope of moral status is extended the greater number of moral conflicts that have to be resolved.

RADICAL ECOLOGICAL ETHICS

Perhaps, extending traditional theories is so difficult because traditional theories are the problem. They fail because moral status for other entities has to be justified by trying to find similarities with humans. But, perhaps what we really need is a *radically new ideological perspective*

Apologies
to Escher

An *ideology* is a set of basic ideas, beliefs and values that influence our moral judgements. If those ideas, beliefs and values are wrong then we have a *distorted ideological perspective*. A distorted ideological perspective might lead us to make false moral judgments. Radical ecological philosophies claim that traditional theories are based on distorted ideological perspectives. So, solving environmental issues requires a new ideological perspective.

There are various forms of radical ecological philosophies that sometimes conflict with each other. But, they all have in common a belief that resolving environmental issues requires a fundamental change to our ideas, beliefs and values regarding the natural world and our place in it. Radical ecological philosophies are often *political* as well as ethical. They claims that environmental issues are connected with other social and political problems. Radical theories thus require not merely ethical changes to our individual behaviour but also political changes to our collective behaviour. They demand changes to social and political institutions.

DEEP ECOLOGY

An important radical ecological philosophy is Deep Ecology. It views the assumption that humans are separate from nature as the major cause of environmental problems. **Arne Næss,** on a visit to the Himalayas was impressed by the way that Sherpa guides treated certain mountains as sacred. Næss advocates extending a similar reverence to all of nature. Deep ecology is ecocentric. It asserts the intrinsic value of human and non-human life and natural objects. It condemns human interference with nature, calls for a substantial decrease in human population and advocates fundamental economic, cultural and political changes.

'Deep' versus 'shallow' ecology

Næss described his new viewpoint as *"**deep ecology**"* in contrast to the *"**shallow ecology**"* of contemporary environmentalism which, he argued, merely seeks technological fixes to environmental issues. By 'shallow ecology', Næss means anthropocentric ethics that attach only instrumental value to non-human entities. Deep ecology, by contrast, is ecocentric. It recognizes the intrinsic value and interdependence of all life, where 'life' is used in a non-technical sense to include landscapes and ecosystems.

Shallow ecology is the "fight against pollution and resource depletion". It is concerned only with "the health and affluence of people in the developed countries."

Deep ecology views all living things as alike in having value in their own right, independent of their usefulness to others. It is concerned with respecting this intrinsic value.

Deep ecologists and 'shallow' environmentalists may advocate different approaches towards solving environmental issues, such as pollution and resource depletion.

There's no need to act on acid rain. We need more research

We should fight the economic conditions causing acid rain

The market will conserve resources. Technology will find substitutes

Do increases in production and consumption satisfy vital needs?

Plants or animals that are of no use to humans do not matter

Resources and habitats for all life-forms matter for their own sake

Overpopulation is a problem for developing countries

Pressure stemming from the industrial societies is a major factor

Western type industrialization is the goal for developing countries

Cultural diversity is a human analogue to biological diversity

Deep Questioning

Deep ecology claims to be "the ecology movement which questions deeper". Anthropocentric arguments for conservation, Naess claims, can get stalled in technical disagreements or weaken motivation to fight for necessary social changes. Deep ecology, by contrast, questions everything, including underlying assumptions, value priorities and beliefs. It questions the goals and viability of industrial societies and their focus on economic growth. But, it can also question some ecocentric claims, such as that humans are 'plain citizens' on a par with all other species with no special obligations to their own species.

Deep ecology involves a willingness to question, and an appreciation of the importance of questioning, every economic and political policy in public.

The Eight Point Platform

Deep Ecology includes an ***eight point platform of basic principles*** that are common to all deep ecological philosophies. Deep ecology is not one particular doctrine. There may be various and diverse deep ecological philosophies. But, they will all have these basic principles in common.

1. The flourishing of human and nonhuman life on earth has inherent value. The value of nonhuman life-forms is independent of the usefulness of the nonhuman world for human purposes.
2. Richness and diversity of life-forms are also values in themselves and contribute to the flourishing of human and nonhuman life on earth.
3. Humans have no fight to reduce this richness and diversity except to satisfy *vital* needs.
4. The flourishing of human life and cultures is compatible with a substantial decrease of the human population. The flourishing of nonhuman life requires such a decrease.
5. Present human interference with the nonhuman world is excessive, and the situation is rapidly worsening.
6. In view of the foregoing points, policies must be changed. The changes in policies affect basic economic, technological, and ideological structures. The resulting state of affairs will be deeply different from the present and make possible a more joyful experience of the connectedness of all things.
7. The ideological change is mainly that of appreciating life quality (dwelling in situations of inherent value) rather than adhering to an increasingly higher standard of living. There will be a profound awareness of the difference between big and great.
8. Those who subscribe to the foregoing points have an obligation directly or indirectly to participate in the attempt to implement the necessary changes.

The principles claim that non-human entities have intrinsic value, and they demand political action to realize those values. Deep ecology is not an academic philosophical system, nor an institutionalised ideology. Different people may have different priorities. "Vital needs" and "quality of life" may mean different things in different cultures and climates. Deep ecologists may support different political parties. But, they will all agree on supporting the same kind of deep ecological lifestyle expressed by the principles. They will all endorse preserving wilderness and biodiversity, controlling human population and living simply. That is, treading lightly on the planet.

A Derivational System

Næss describes deep ecology as a "**derivational system**" that can be used by different religious and philosophical systems, such as Buddhism, Christianity or analytical philosophy. Different philosophical systems will stop deep questioning at different **ultimate premises** that cannot be questioned further. From these ultimate premises they each logically derive **general principles** and **particular rules**. They may each derive different principles and rules, but all deep ecological systems will include the eight-point platform principles. According to Naess, shallow environmentalism is not linked to ultimate premises. So, environmentalist policy 'oughts' are not derived from 'oughts' in ultimate premises. So, we cannot be sure that they are rational. The deep ecological platform however, ensures that policies are logically derived.

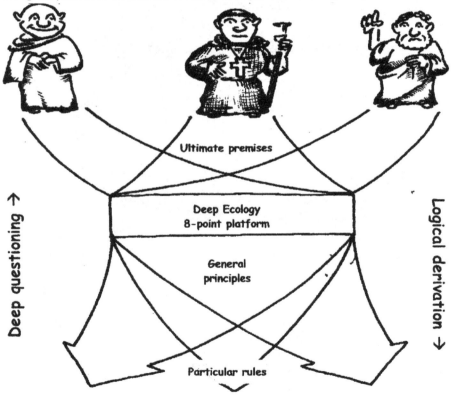

Ecosophy

The deep ecological platform can be used with multiple ultimate premises and allows the derivation of multiple ecological philosophies, or **ecosophies**. We need a new ecosophy, Naess argues, to replace current destructive views of industrial societies that see themselves as separate from nature. An ecosophy is **descriptive** and **normative**. That is, it describes facts about the world and also provides **norms**, standards that tell us how we ought to behave. Facts about the world can change, and we may each derive different norms from our own ultimate premises. So, there can be many different possible ecosophies.

By an ecosophy I mean a philosophy of ecological harmony or equilibrium.

Ecosophy T

Næss's own preferred ecological philosophy **"Ecosophy T"** is named after his Tvergastein mountain cabin where it was developed. Ecosophy T combines elements from **Buddhism** with the methods of nonviolent action of **Gandhi** and the unified total worldview of **Spinoza**.

I believe in the essential unity of man and ... of all that lives

Unity of nature means that everything is connected to everything else and that therefore the self-realization of one living being is part of the self-realization of all other beings

Ecosophy T advocates *friluftsliv*, open-air life, and outdoor recreation enjoying nature for its own sake. Næss's guidelines for *friluftsliv* include respect for all life, respect for landscape, outdoor education, minimal strain upon nature, natural lifestyle, and time for adjustment.

Self-Realization!

The primary norm of Ecosophy T is **Self-realization!** The capital 'S' indicates not the narrow egoistic self, but an expanded **ecological Self** that identifies with "the living earth". The exclamation mark indicates that it is a norm, something we should aim to achieve. If conservation is seen as a moral duty involving sacrifice of egoistic self-interest then it does not have a very reliable base. But, identification with nature makes conservation a matter of ecological Self-interest. Næss loosely defines self-realization as the fulfilment of our potentialities. As we mature, we learn that by realizing a 'social self' that shares with others we fulfil more potentialities than can our egoistical self alone. Næss proposes that we would fulfil greater and richer potentialities by realizing a wider and deeper 'ecological self' that identifies with nature. That is, a self that recognizes that it is not separate from nature, a self that sees itself in other living things.

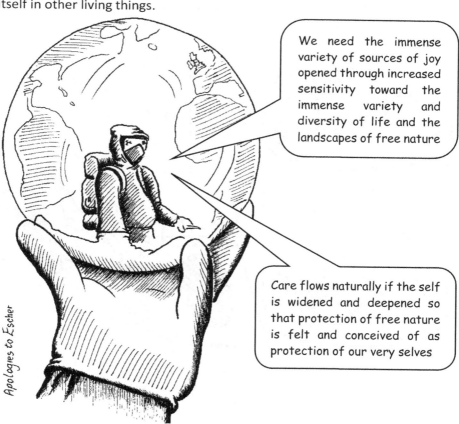

We need the immense variety of sources of joy opened through increased sensitivity toward the immense variety and diversity of life and the landscapes of free nature

Care flows naturally if the self is widened and deepened so that protection of free nature is felt and conceived of as protection of our very selves

Apologies to Escher

Total View

We all have a **total view** of the world, Næss claims, which includes basic attitudes and practical decisions to act in certain ways. Næss rejects the view that we are isolated individuals separated from nature. Organisms are not isolated objects **defined in** their environment, but are partly **defined by** their environment. That is, individuals are partly defined as **nodes in a biospherical network** or **total field** of intrinsic relationships with all other organisms and ecosystems in the biosphere. If those relationships change then the individual organism changes. Our environment partly determines what we are. We are integral parts of our environment, essentially connected to each other and the rest of nature.

Our basic attitudes influence our practical decisions. An isolated egoistical self will see conservation as a sacrifice to moral duty. But, if we see ourselves as essentially interrelated to each other and to the rest of nature then, Næss argues, we will feel greater empathy and concern for other beings and nature generally. Self-realization thus makes conservation not merely a moral duty but a matter of (expanded) Self-interest. If we realize how much our own well-being depends on the well-being of nature then we will be more strongly motivated to protect non-human life and nature generally.

The attempt to ignore our dependence ... has contributed to the alienation of man from himself

Biospherical Egalitarianism

If we view ourselves as nodes in a biospherical network of relationships we may decide to endorse *biospherical egalitarianism*. Næss argues that we will recognize the intrinsic value of all other nodes in the total network. We will see that we have no privileged place, that all beings are striving for self-realization, unfolding their own potentials in their own ways. We will then see that all living things have equal intrinsic value and an equal right to live and flourish, regardless of their usefulness to others.

N.B. Næss acknowledges that biospherical egalitarianism holds *in principle*. 'In principle' because in real life some killing or exploitation may be necessary. We need to eat and protect ourselves from disease.)

Transpersonal Ecology

Warwick Fox developed self-realization into **_transpersonal ecology_**. That is, we should attempt to realize an _ecological consciousness_ that tries to identify as widely as possible with the rest of the non-human world. He argued that it is too unrealistic to claim that nature has intrinsic value then devise moral principles to respect this value. Our moral self will be in continual conflict with our egoistic self. If instead we develop an **_ecological consciousness_** that recognizes that we and all other beings are aspects of a single unfolding reality, then moral principles will become unnecessary. Our ecological consciousness will want to protect the environment in order to protect our own selves.

Ethics is rendered superfluous. If one has a wide expansive sense of self then one will naturally protect the unfolding of this expansive self (the ecosphere, the cosmos) in all its aspects

Questions for Deep Ecology
Does deep ecology have totalitarian implications?

As with Leopold's land ethic, it might be argued that individual interests should be subordinated to the greater good of the biotic community. For example, some activists in the *Earth First!* movement used deep ecology concepts to justify violent action, and argue for an end to food aid to starving people.

Supporters of deep ecology reject the charge of totalitarianism. It endorses diversity, "the more diversity the better". They can also respond that it is a long range movement. Although deep ecology advocates population reduction, this could be achieved by voluntary methods over centuries.

Is deep ecology too vague to address real environmental issues?

Some critics argue that the eight point platform is too vague. It does not tell us precisely what to do, nor how to resolve moral conflicts. Supporters of deep ecology may respond that it is about developing an ecological worldview, not devising moral rules. But, how do we show equal respect to all living things? Even with an appropriate ecological consciousness, we would still need principles to resolve conflicts. Moreover, without principles what should people who do not develop an ecological consciousness be expected to do?

The well-being and flourishing of human and nonhuman life on Earth have value in themselves

What, even disease-causing organisms?

We don't say that every living being has the same value as a human, but that it has an intrinsic value which is not quantifiable ... I may kill a mosquito if it is on the face of my baby but I will never say I have a higher right to life than a mosquito

Is Deep Ecology elitist?

Some third world critics accuse deep ecology of attempting to preserve wilderness areas for those few with the wealth and leisure to enjoy them. **Ramachandra Guha**, for example, describes the actions of western conservation groups as a new form of cultural imperialism.

Næss himself sees deep ecology as one of three great movements, along with peace and social justice. The three are linked. For example, environmental issues have the worst effects on the poorest people. Solutions would be labour-intensive, so could reduce unemployment. Moreover, the eight-point platform allows wide cultural diversity. Self-determination and local community are among deep ecology's key terms. Nevertheless, global action is also increasingly necessary. So, how should deep ecological principles be applied locally? And how should they be balanced against global actions?

Could identification with nature justify exploitation of nature?

It might be argued that I am entitled to treat myself in any way I like. I identify with nature. So, I will treat nature in any way I like. **Val Plumwood** argued that Self-realization could be interpreted in different ways, all of which fail to recognize differences between individuals, and so fail to give others their due.

If self-realization means viewing the self as indistinguishable from nature, it could justify exploitation as well as conservation.

If self-realization means impartially identifying with *all* of nature, it cannot account for the attachment that many indigenuous peoples and conservationists feel for the land.

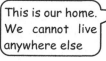

This is our home. We cannot live anywhere else

If self-realization means empathizing with as many beings as possible, it could mean an expansion of egoism that fails to recognize the differing needs of others.

133

It is now widely agreed that humans are more deeply interconnected with nature than was previously thought. But, it is still not clear what 'identification with nature' might mean. Not all environmentalists would endorse all of the eight-point platform principles. And, I'm not sure there is a strict division between 'deep' and 'shallow' ecology.

Yes, it is now more usual to talk about a **spectrum** of viewpoints, ranging from light to dark or deep green. Moreover, deep ecology is still **male-centred**. It is mostly concerned with conserving 'wilderness'. But, in a patriarchal society who decides what constitutes wilderness? Feminist analysis provides another radical viewpoint.

ECOFEMINISM

Ecofeminism ("ecological feminism") applies feminist analysis to ecological issues. The term was first coined in 1974 by **Françoise d'Eaubonne** who argued that both the domination of women and the exploitation of nature result from the male domination of society.

> The oppressive social structures that justify the domination and exploitation of women also justify the domination and exploitation of nature.

There are many feminist views, and many views on nature. There are therefore many different ecofeminist views. But, they all generally agree that there are important connections between the domination of women and the exploitation of nature. The connections that feminist analysis has revealed may be **empirical, historical and symbolic**.

Empirical Connections

Many feminists point out the *empirical evidence* connecting the dominations of women and of nature. For example, **Ariel Salleh** criticizes "*patriarchal economics*" which ignores most work performed by women.

Governments base decisions on **GDP** (Gross Domestic Product). But GDP does not include the unpaid household work that is mostly performed by women. Putting a value on unpaid work is difficult. But, estimates range from about 50% to 80% of GDP.

Empirical evidence also suggests that environmental issues have the worst effects on women, children, ethnic minorities and the poorest people.

The World Bank says that in the developing world, of the 1.6 billion who live in extreme poverty the majority are women. Women are more concentrated in subsistence agriculture while men dominate wage and formal sector employment

The World Health Organization says that children suffer a disproportionate share of environmental health burdens

Historical Connections

Some ecofeminists point out historical connections between the domination of women and of nature. Nature has traditionally been thought of as female, and women thought of as closer to nature. **Carolyn Merchant** believes there was an older world order based on an *organic metaphor* of nature and cooperation between humans and nature.

Nature was seen as female organic and nurturing

If nature is seen as a nurturing beneficent female then destructive acts against nature would be seen as unethical. But, the scientific revolution replaced the organic metaphor of nature with the mechanistic world view of modern science. Because nature was now viewed as a system of dead inert particles ... the mechanical framework itself could legitimate the manipulation of nature.

THE DEATH OF NATURE

PLASTIC FLOWERS

Merchant suggests that people used to live in close-knit, cooperative, organic communities until the *scientific revolution* replaced the organic metaphor with the *mechanistic metaphor.* The new machine metaphor redefined reality and justified rational control over nature, society and the self.

Symbolic Connections

Ecofeminists also point out the **symbolic connections** between the devaluation of women and nature in religion, art and literature. For example, Merchant describes the use of language that treats women as 'natural' and nature as 'female'. She discusses the **female metaphors** used to justify the domination of nature used by **Francis Bacon (1561-1626)**, 'father of science'. 'Mother' nature's secrets are 'penetrated'. Her 'womb' contains 'many secrets of excellent use' to the 'man of science'. There are many examples of gendered language connecting women and nature, 'virgin' timber, fertile' soil, 'barren' land, and so on and on.

139

The Great Chain of Being

Some ecofeminists agree that women have a special connection to nature. They argue that women have important cultural and spiritual relationships with the earth that are respected by some indigenous cultures. Some also argue that the justification for ignoring women's special connection is the 'Great Chain of Being', a patriarchal hierarchy that separates God from Man and Man from women, children, animals, plans and rocks*.

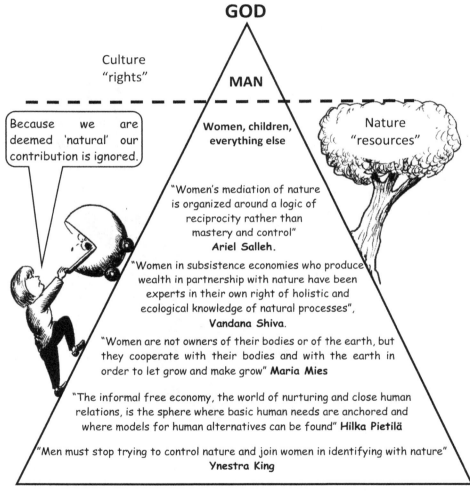

GOD

Culture
"rights"

MAN

Because we are deemed 'natural' our contribution is ignored.

Women, children, everything else

Nature
"resources"

"Women's mediation of nature is organized around a logic of reciprocity rather than mastery and control"
Ariel Salleh.

"Women in subsistence economies who produce wealth in partnership with nature have been experts in their own right of holistic and ecological knowledge of natural processes",
Vandana Shiva.

"Women are not owners of their bodies or of the earth, but they cooperate with their bodies and with the earth in order to let grow and make grow" **Maria Mies**

"The informal free economy, the world of nurturing and close human relations, is the sphere where basic human needs are anchored and where models for human alternatives can be found" **Hilka Pietilä**

"Men must stop trying to control nature and join women in identifying with nature"
Ynestra King

*diagram adapted from Ariel Salleh in *Working with Nature: Reciprocity or Control*.

The Rationalist Tradition

Not all ecofeminists agree that women have a special connection to nature. Another viewpoint is that the dominations of both women and nature derive from the male-biased concepts of the Classical Greek **rationalist tradition**.

> The **rationalist tradition** uses damaging assumptions that are not only biased from a gender perspective, but have claimed a negative role for nature as well

NO POLITICAL ANIMALS

Val Plumwood argues that conceptual structures of domination construct women and nature in male-biased ways. These conceptual structures are based on **value dualisms** and **value hierarchies**.

> **Value dualism** splits things into opposing pairs

> **Value hierarchy** grants higher status to one of each pair

Examples include mind/body, reason/emotion, human/nature and male/female. So, anything associated with mind, reason, human and male is superior to anything associated with body, emotion, nature and female.

Oppressive Conceptual Frameworks

Karen Warren argues that value dualism and hierarchy need not be harmful. They become harmful when they support *oppressive conceptual frameworks*. Value dualism merely lists differences. But if it is claimed that one side is morally inferior, then it can be used to justify oppression of that which is deemed morally inferior.

Conceptual frameworks are sets of basic beliefs, values and assumptions that shape the way we see the world

Oppressive conceptual frameworks justify and maintain unjust relationships of domination and oppression

Patriarchal oppressive conceptual frameworks justify the subordination of women by men

The Logic of Domination

Oppressive conceptual frameworks involve an unjust *logic of domination*. That is, ethical premises used to justify oppression. Warren argues that a patriarchal conceptual framework uses a similar logic of domination to justify the oppression both of women and of nature.

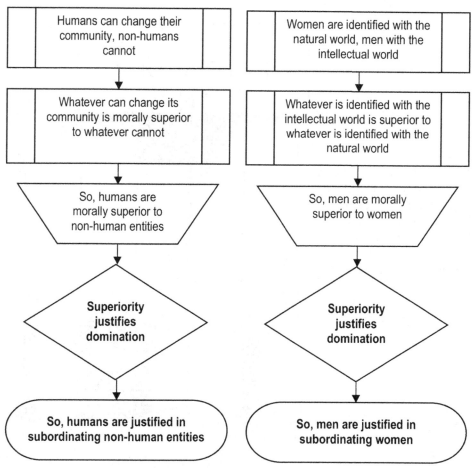

Most ecofeminists reject one or both of the first two premises. All reject the fourth premise. Feminists and environmentalists thus share the common goal of abolishing this oppressive conceptual framework.

The same logic of domination is used to justify other forms of oppression, Warren also argues, such as racism, classism, ageism, and heterosexism. Ecofeminists reject this logic. So, they are opposed to all forms of oppression. Ecofeminists generally accept an argument made previously by **Sheila Collins** that patriarchy is supported by four interlocking pillars: sexism, racism, class exploitation, and ecological destruction.

144

Oppressive Dualisms

Modern attempts to extend traditional ethics to include the environment may still make use of the male-biased rationalist tradition. Val Plumwood argues that Tom Regan's attempt to extend rights to non-human animals and Paul Taylor's recognition of inherent worth still incorporate oppressive dualisms. They oppose reason to emotion. But, this leads to absurd conclusions, such as the impartial defence of the rights of both predators and prey.

Moreover, the anthropocentrism of the Western tradition may be founded on these oppressive dualisms. The dualistic account opposes reason to emotion, masculine to feminine, public to private and so on. So, extending rationalist ethical theories merely perpetuates the value dualisms and hierarchies that are the root cause of environmental problems.

146

The "discontinuity thesis"

Plumwood argues that the problem with patriarchal value dualism is that it defines the human self as ***discontinuous***, separate and different from nature.

This leads to a view of humans as apart from nature, usually as masters or external controllers of it

What is virtuous in the human is taken to be what maximizes distance from the merely natural

The relation of humans to nature is treated as an oppositional value dualism

The features that are taken to be characteristic of humankind ... are those such as rationality, freedom and transcendence of nature (all traditionally viewed as masculinnnnnnnnnnnneee ...

The Relational Self

Ecofeminism agrees with Deep Ecology that the self is interrelated with society and nature. They disagree however about the nature of the relationship. According to Plumwood, Deep Ecoogy's 'realized Self' fails to respect differences. But, ecofeminism's relational self is at the same time an individual with morally significant individual experiences, beliefs and desires. Ecofeminism thus regards individual rights as well as relationships with other individuals and with society and nature as morally significant. So, caring for nature is a moral duty, though this care may be expressed in different ways.

Some ecofeminists endorse
environmental virtue ethics.

Some ecofeminists endorse
environmental justice.

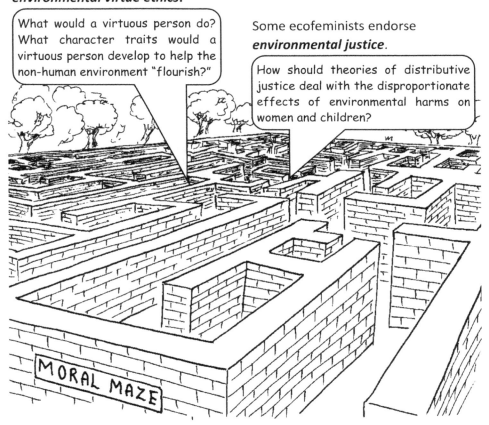

What would a virtuous person do? What character traits would a virtuous person develop to help the non-human environment "flourish?"

How should theories of distributive justice deal with the disproportionate effects of environmental harms on women and children?

MORAL MAZE

Care Ethics

Many ecofeminists endorse *care ethics*. Psychologist **Carol Gilligan** and philosopher **Nell Noddings** argued that 'feminine' moral reasoning, based on caring for others, provided a "*different voice*" from the traditional 'masculine' voice of justice. Justice is concerned with individual rights and liberties. It appeals to rational, universal and impartial rules. Care ethics is concerned with care and empathy for others. It appeals to "emotional intelligence" and maintaining harmonious relationships. Care ethics is thus similar to moral sentiments and virtue ethics.

Justice-based theories attempt to identify a qualifying property for moral status. Non-human entities that have that property must be treated justly. Care ethics bases moral status on relational attitudes humans have or could have towards others. Parents can love their children unconditionally, regardless of any properties those children may or may not possess. By analogy with the care of parents for their children, ecofeminist care ethicists argue that humans can learn to care for non-human animals and nature as an expression of a relational attitude, not because of any qualifying properties. Moreover, our own health and the health of nature depend on our caring about non-human animals and nature. We are interrelated with the rest of the natural world. Interrelatedness gives us a duty of care. So, we have a duty to deepen our understanding and extend our sense of care to the natural world.

150

Questions for Ecofeminism
Is ecofeminism *essentialist*?

To claim that women have a special connection with nature assumes that men and women are **essentially different**. That is, man and women have different essential characteristics that make them what they are. But, most feminists argue that there are no essential differences between men and women.

Some ecofeminists do indeed believe that men and women are essentially different. But, they claim that their special connection with nature makes women better constituted to rebuild our relationship with the natural world. Some also adopt a spiritualist view that regards nature as female and sacred. Rebuilding our relationship to nature requires changes to individual beliefs.

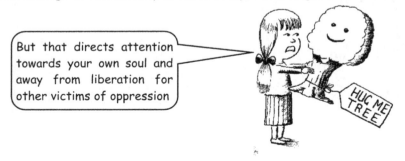

Most ecofeminists however, deny that women and men are essentially different. They agree that purported differences between men and women are socially conditioned. Nevertheless, they argue that even though socially conditioned, this connection to nature is vital, for both men and women.

Is Ecofeminism anti-intellectual?

Critics argue that rationalism need not promote oppression. Even if rationalism implies dualism, it is only harmful if it is associated with superiority. Moreover, rationalism may be the best means of countering domination. Furthermore, care and moral sentiments are too unreliable to provide a basis for ethics. Parents can express care for their children in morally blameworthy ways.

In response, ecofeminists can argue that they have constructed rationalist arguments against domination. Moreover, not all ecofeminists endorse care ethics, and those that do argue that it is complementary to justice, not a replacement. An ability to care is essential to moral reasoning, and the best way to express care is a matter of reason. For example, how parents care for their children can be a matter of moral evaluation, subject to praise or blame.

SOCIAL ECOLOGY

Another radical view is that ecological problems originate in social problems.

Murray Bookchin argues that social hierarchy and human domination have led to a belief in natural hierarchy in which nature is separate from humans and can be dominated. He argues that prehistoric human societies were largely egalitarian. But, as populations increased and societies became more complex they also become more hierarchical. Hierarchical societies eventually produced elite ruling classes, usually male elites who dominate women and other men. Population growth, natural disasters and technological changes privileged male activities of hunting over the horticultural functions of females.

Developments in technology and means of production gave greater power to the marketplace. Bookchin argues that the market produces and distributes goods and services for profit rather than mutual aid. Market-based societies are inherently competitive. They pit humans against each other and against the rest of the natural world. Humans are converted into commodities, and similarly nature is "converted into a commodity, a resource to be manufactured and merchandised wantonly". Moreover, because capitalism is committed to continual economic growth, it cannot solve environmental problems caused by growth. For example, if population numbers could be reduced the remaining population would have to increase consumption in order to maintain economic growth. Continual growth requires continually increasing consumption regardless of by how many people.

Bookchin advocates replacing the free market ideology that has reduced humans and the rest of nature to mere commodities. If instead we see ourselves as part of a continually evolving process, from simple single-celled to increasingly intelligent organisms, we would reject the anthropocentric view that we are separate from nature, and the biocentric view that we are parasites on nature. If we see ourselves as "**nature rendered conscious**", we would replace exploitation with preservation of nature.

Humans are a product of a significant evolutionary trend toward intellectuality, self-awareness, will, intentionality, and expressiveness.

Bookchin describes our biological evolutionary history as "**first nature**". Humans also have a "**second nature**", our ability to cooperate in lage societies. Humans are no different to other species in striving to meet our first nature needs. But, our second nature gives us greater ability to alter our environment to meet those needs. However, second nature also gives us the potential either to develop an ecological society or to destroy the biosphere.

Liberation of both humans and nature depend on each other. Bookchin argues that humans must recognize that we are part of the unfolding process of nature and should act to support that unfolding. We should help to maintain complexity and diversity, and aim to minimize suffering and pollution. Instead of acting against nature, we should act as if we were nature rendered conscious. Human societies and relationships with the rest of nature could be modelled on the non-hierarchical relationships found in nature. Bookchin proposes small local communities, based on sustainable agriculture, democratic participation and freedom from domination.

159

Bioregionalism

Bioregionalism is the view that human communities should be integrated with their regional ecologies. **Lewis Mumford** is the main influence for this view. He argued that a runaway industrial capitalist *"megamachine"* uses humans as resources and reduces the planets capacity to support life. *Bioregions* are defined by natural boundaries such as watersheds, or by characteristic types of terrain. *Bioregionalists* advocate *'reinhabitation',* learning to inhabit a bioregion. Reinhabitation involves becoming members of a region's biotic community and developing our potential within its ecological limits. Instead of a homogenous consumer culture, bioregional communities would consume local foods, use local materials, grow native plants, and encourage sustainability within the bioregion.

The Tragedy of the Commons

The '***tragedy of the commons***' illustrates the connection between social and environmental problems. According to the ecologist **Garret Hardin**, resources held in common tend to become depleted. Suppose a group of farmers are each entitled to graze their cattle on a commonly owned area of land. It is in each farmer's self-interest to graze as many cattle as possible. The farmer gains the benefit, while the community bears the cost. But, if all farmers make the same choice, the commons becomes overused, and all become worse off.

There are many examples of such ***collective action problems***, where individual actions might not cause much harm, but if everyone does them the collective consequences can be significantly harmful. A fishing vessel can take "one more catch" without causing much harm. But, if all fishing vessels take one more catch then fish stocks collapse. "One more" car will not add much pollution, but if everyone drives then pollution escalates uncontrollably. And so on.

Property Rights

Most previously common land has now been **enclosed**. That is, taken into private ownership. But, the air and the sea are still part of a **global commons**, global resources shared internationally. Advocates of free markets argue that adequate **property rights** would solve the tragedy of the global commons. Owners would take better care of privately owned resources from which they can profit. Polluters would be held legally responsible for the harmful consequences of their actions. The **free market** would achieve the greatest good for the greatest number. Governments should be restricted to protecting individual liberties and property rights which would include monitoring pollution and enforcing liablity for damages to individual rights or liberties.

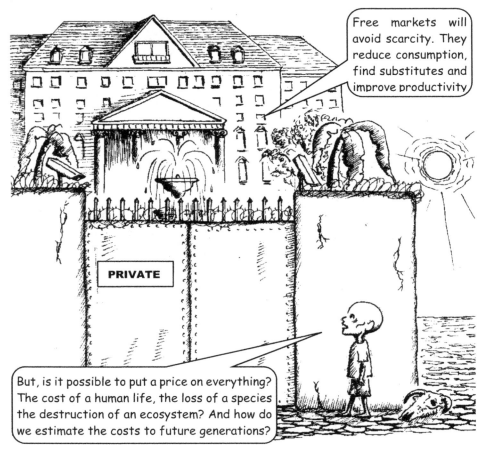

Ecosystem Services

Some scientists, economists and environmentalists have attempted to put a price on *ecosystem services*. Ecosystems provide many 'services', or benefits, to humans, such as providing food and water, or controlling climate and disease. But, ecosystem services are being degraded because they are assumed to be unlimited and free. However if these services could be given a price, policy-makers might be better able to take them into account when making decisions that affect the environment.

But, can you commodify nature? Do ecosystems have other values besides merely economic value? Can all ecosystem services be given a price?

Market Failures

Many people believe unregulated markets are themselves the problem. Environmental problems are often a result of **market failures**. Ideal market conditions should achieve the most efficient distribution of resources, in theory. In practice, we do not have these ideal conditions. So, real world markets often fail to allocate resources efficiently. One important type of market failure is **negative externalities,** external costs imposed on third parties. In the ideal market, costs are met privately between buyers and sellers. But, in the real world there are often costs imposed on others. For example, cars are privately owned, but the costs of traffic congestion and pollution are paid for by society as a whole. Market **supply and demand** is based only on private cost. But, if this private cost is less than the full (private plus social) cost then markets produce more of the product. So, markets tend to **overproduce** negative externalites, such as pollution. And the biggest negative externality of all time is climate change.

Green Taxes

Ameliorating market failures requires government intervention, either by regulations or by taxes. Some environmentalists endorse **green taxes**. Green taxes are examples of **Pigouvian taxes**. The economist **A. C. Pigou** suggested that taxes could **internalize the costs of externalities**. A green tax would add the external social cost to the producers internal private cost. The market cost would then reflect the true full cost. Producers and consumers would then have to take into account the social costs, such as pollution. This solution would avoid the need for government regulations, and allow the free market to resolve environmental problem. However, it is important to note that it would not eliminate pollution. It would reduce pollution to an 'optimum' level, where the costs of reducing pollution further would outweigh the benefits.

Critics argue that green taxes are *regressive*. The costs are passed on to customers. But poorer people spend proportionally more than the rich on energy and heating. So, poorer people would bear a disproportionate burden in paying the costs of green taxes.

In response, it could be argued that redistributing some of the revenue could make green taxes progressive. It could also be argued that green taxes benefit poorer people who cannot 'buy their way out' of environmental issues.

Thanks to emissions trading, we can buy our way out of environmental responsibility

But, how do you set green taxes to the correct level without distorting the market further? Some forms of pollution may be too dangerous to leave to the market. In some cases regulations may be more efficient, and safer.

Government Regulations

Some environmentalists argue that **government regulations** are necessary to solve environmental issues. Many environmentalists reject market solutions because they assume everything has only instrumental value. But some things, such as safe drinking water or breathable air, have intrinsic value. They are too valuable to bargain away. Mitigating environmental damage therefore, should be a matter of **public debate** and **political decisions**. In practice however, environmental policies generally involve some mix of market solutions and government regulations.

Democratic Planning

Many argue that capitalism itself is the problem and that **democratic planning** is necessary to solve environmental issues. James O'Connor points out the contradiction that capitalism is committed to continual growth while at the same time undermining the environmental and labour conditions necessary to sustain continual growth. Solving environmental problems, he argues, requires a democratically organized socialist state, which controls the division of labour and centrally manages protection of the environment.

The externalization of social and environmental costs has resulted in a deterioration of environmental and labour conditions

Social and environmental issues are global issues pertaining to the way that money capital is allocated worldwide, and thus require globally coordinated political action

TRICKLE DOWN

apologies to Millet

Questions for Social Ecology

Should societies be guided by nature?

Like ecocentric ethics, social ecology has to answer the questions raised by John Stuart Mill. If nature is often hostile to human life and values then should we be guided by nature? What do we mean by nature? How do we distinguish natural and artificial?

Is social ecology too anthropocentric?

If social ecology is anthropocentric then it may fail to grant the natural world its due moral standing. Bookchin argues that humans must support the unfolding of nature. But is nature unfolding in any particular direction? If it is, can we assume that humans have any significant place in this unfolding?

Which natural features should define bioregions, and why?

Would social ecological solutions take too long?

Some environmentalists criticize social ecology for focussing on long-term social change without short-term solutions for current environmental issues.

So, social ecology seems correct in that the current capitalist system is unsustainable. Free markets overproduce negative externalities, such as pollution. And there is evidence that these externalities have already exceeded some of the planet's ecological limits
It also seems widely accepted that markets need some regulations. All nations currently regulate markets to some extent, though the appropriate extent of regulation is still a matter of debate
NO SMOKING

ENVIRONMENTAL POLITICS

Environmental ethics is clearly an important study in itself. But, it is also connected to a wide range of other disciplines. It is clearly connected to politics, for example. Ethics asks how we should live as individuals. But, it also makes claims about how we believe the world ought to be. And changing the world requires **political action**. For example, global political cooperation is required to mitigate global problems, such as climate change. So, politics and ethics interact. Politics raises ethical questions about what are the right policies to implement, and ethics raises political questions about what we should do as individuals and what we should expect from the state.

ENVIRONMENTAL JUSTICE

Environmental problems raise many ethical and political questions concerning human rights and distributive justice.

Human rights to life, liberty and personal security, are often compromised by environmental problems. For example, climate change is causing significant increases in the rates of death and disease, especially in the poorest countries.

Environmental justice is concered with the equitable distribution of environmental risks and benefits. The richest tend to contribute most to overconsumption, pollution and climate change, while the poorest suffer the worst effects.

ENVIRONMENTAL HUMANITIES

Environmental humanities is an emerging interdisciplinary area of research that studies the relations between humans and their environment. It combines approaches from various disciplines, such as philosophy, literature, art, history and anthropology. It also draws on traditional approaches from various parts of the world, as well as western viewpoints. It studies, for example, the historical development of concepts of "nature" and the role of humans in those concepts. It also studies the ways in which those concepts are changing. Many of the subjects of study in environmental humanities involve questions of value which, of course, is the subject of environmental ethics.

ENVIRONMENTAL SCIENCE

Environmental ethics is obviously also connected to science. Science made possible the technology that contributes to environmental problems. But, science also makes discoveries about the environment and provides evidence of the harm that we are causing. Science will also have to be involved in finding solutions to environmental problems. At the same time, scientists might disagree about interpretations of data or solutions. But, these disagreement are often based on disagreements about questions of ethical value.

BIBLIOGRAPHY

The text of this book is largely drawn from the sources listed here. Needless to say, any errors are all mine.

Belshaw, Christopher. *Environmental philosophy*. McGill-Queen's Press-MQUP, 2001.

Benson, John. *Environments, Ethics and Human Concern*. Open University, 1999.

Brennan, Andrew and Lo, Yeuk-Sze, "Environmental Ethics", *The Stanford Encyclopedia of Philosophy* (Winter 2015 Edition), Edward N. Zalta (ed).

Cochrane, Alasdair. "Environmental ethics." *Internet encyclopedia of philosophy* 2006.

Gruen, Lori, "The Moral Status of Animals", *The Stanford Encyclopedia of Philosophy* (Fall 2014 Edition), Edward N. Zalta (ed.).

Hursthouse, Rosalind. *Humans and other animals*. Open University, 2000.

Leopold, Aldo. *A sand county almanac*. New York 1949.

Naess, Arne. *Ecology of Wisdom*. Penguin, 2008.

Regan, Tom. *The case for animal rights*. Univ of California Press, 2004.

Singer, Peter (ed.). *A Companion to Ethics. Blackwell Publishing, 2012.*

Singer, Peter. *Animal liberation*. Random House, 1995.

Taylor, Paul W. *Respect for nature: A theory of environmental ethics*. Princeton University Press, 2011.

Warren, Karen J., "Feminist Environmental Philosophy", *The Stanford Encyclopedia of Philosophy* (Summer 2015 Edition), Edward N. Zalta (ed.).

Zimmerman, Michael E.; Callicott, J. Baird; Sessions, George; Warren, Karen J.; and Clark, John (eds.), *Environmental Philosophy: From Animal Rights to Radical Ecology*, (New Jersey: Prentice Hall, 2nd ed., 1998).

Made in the USA
Monee, IL
06 November 2019